Portraits in Music 2

David Jenkins
Callendar Park College of Education, Falkirk

Mark Visocchi
Notre Dame College of Education, Glasgow

Oxford University Press
Music Department, Ely House, 37 Dover Street, London W1X 4AH

ACKNOWLEDGEMENTS

We are grateful to the following for permission to reproduce copyright material:

Music extracts

Boosey & Hawkes Music Publishers Ltd. (*The Stars and Stripes Forever* by John Philip Sousa and *Petrushka* by Stravinsky); Chappell & Co. Ltd. (*West Side Story,* music by Leonard Bernstein, words by Stephen Sondheim © 1957 Leonard Bernstein and Stephen Sondheim. Original Publisher: G. Schirmer Inc. & Chappell & Co. Inc., British Publisher: Chappell Music Ltd.); J & W Chester/Edition Wilhelm Hansen London Limited (Symphony No. 2 'The Four Temperaments' by Carl Nielsen); Editions Salabert (*Pacific 231* by Arthur Honegger, Copyright by Editions Maurice Senart 1924, Editions Salabert, 22, rue Chauchat, Paris).

Illustrations

p.4 (left) Faber, (right) Hulton Picture Library (2); p.5 Hulton Picture Library (2); p.7 Mansell Collection; p.8 (left) Mansell Collection, (right) Hulton Picture Library; p.9 Mansell Collection; p.10 Roger-Viollet; p.11 Hulton Picture Library; p.12 (left) Hulton Picture Library; p.13 National Film Archive (2); p.14 (left) Bettmann Archive; p.18 Hulton Picture Library (2); p.21 (left) Archiv für Kunst und Geschichte, (top right) Mansell Collection, (bottom right) Hulton Picture Library; p.22 Hulton Picture Library; p.23 Mansell Collection (3); p.24 Archiv für Kunst und Geschichte (3); p.25 Hulton Picture Library (2); p.26 (left) Mansell Collection, (right) Hulton Picture Library; p.27 Archiv für Kunst und Geschichte (2); p.29 (left) Deutsche Grammophon, (right) National Film Archive; p.30 National Film Archive (4); p.32 Archiv für Kunst und Geschichte (2); p.34 (left) Archiv für Kunst und Geschichte, (right) Mansell Collection; p.35 (left) Mansell Collection, (right) Bettmann Archive; p.36 Bettmann Archive; p.39 (left) Roger-Viollet, (right) Photo Bulloz; p.41 Hulton Picture Library; p.43 (left) Hulton Picture library, (right) Mansell Collection; p.45 Archiv für Kunst und Geschichte (2); p.47 (left) Mansell Collection, (right) Hulton Picture Library; p.48 (left) Hulton Picture Library, (right) Donald Southern; p.50 Donald Southern; p.51 Mansell Collection (2); p.53 and p.54 Archiv für Kunst und Geschichte; p.55 Bettmann Archive (2); p.57 and p.58 Roger Wood; p.59 Mansell Collection (2); p.61 Archiv für Kunst und Geschichte (top), Mansell Collection.

The illustration of the piano on page 42 is by Roger Gorringe and the other instruments are by Constance Dear.

ANSWERS TO 'QUIZ' QUESTIONS 7 AND 8

7. (a) Whither? (The Fair Maid of the Mill); (b) Spartacus; (c) Petrushka; (d) Symphony No. 9 in E minor (From the New World).
8. Tam O' Shanter; Maria; The Vienna Woods; 'Weel done, Cutty-sark'; 'Steal away'; Chaos.

TO PAUL DAVID

© Oxford University Press 1981

All rights reserved. No part of this publication may be reproduced, stored in a retrieval system, or transmitted, in any form or by any means, electronic, mechanical, photocopying, recording, or otherwise, without the prior permission of Oxford University Press.

First published 1981

ISBN 0 19 321401 6

In the same series

Portraits in Music 1

Designed and typeset by AP Graphics, Tonbridge
Printed in England by West Central Printing Co. Ltd., London & Suffolk

CONTENTS

		Page	Discography
1.	Overture *Tam O'Shanter* by Malcolm Arnold (b. 1921)	4	SPA 175
2.	Two movements from *Fantastic Symphony* by Hector Berlioz (1803-1869)	8	ASD 3496
3.	Adagio from *Spartacus* by Aram Khachaturian (1903-1978)	12	ASD 3347
4.	March *The Stars and Stripes Forever* by John Philip Sousa (1854-1932)	14	PFS 4134
5.	*Pacific 231* by Arthur Honegger (1892-1955)	18	ASD 2989
6.	Orchestral prelude from *The Creation* by Joseph Haydn (1732-1809)	21	SLS 5125
7.	Serenade from *Don Giovanni* by Wolfgang Amadeus Mozart (1756-1791)	24	CFP 40246
8.	'Whither?' from *The Fair Maid of the Mill* by Franz Schubert (1797-1828)	26	2530 544
9.	*West Side Story* by Leonard Bernstein (b. 1918)	29	2535 210
10.	Prelude to *The Mastersingers* by Richard Wagner (1813-1883)	32	2537 041
11.	Symphony No. 9 in E minor (From the New World) by Antonín Dvořák (1841-1904)	35	9500 511
12.	Polonaise in A flat major, op. 53 by Frédéric Chopin (1810-1849)	39	2530 659
13.	*Tales from the Vienna Woods* by Johann Strauss II (1825-1899)	43	CFP 40256
14.	*The Bartered Bride* by Bedřich Smetana (1824-1884)	47	SUAST 50397-9
15.	Piano Concerto No. 5 in E flat major (Emperor) by Ludwig van Beethoven (1770-1827)	51	SXL 6899
16.	*Petrushka* by Igor Stravinsky (1882-1971)	55	9500 447 (1947 version of the score)
17.	Chorale Prelude *Through Adam's Fall* by Johann Sebastian Bach (1685-1750)	59	D120D3
18.	Symphony No. 2 (The Four Temperaments) by Carl Nielsen (1865-1931)	62	RHS 325

NOTE TO THE TEACHER

Portraits in Music 2 is a collection of background material to be used in conjunction with 18 pieces of music for listening. While the music has been chosen carefully for its liveliness and general appeal, the depth of treatment which it will receive will depend on the needs and abilities of the class. The books can be used with secondary school pupils of any age following courses in which music listening plays a part. They will be particularly useful supplementary material for pupils in their fourth or fifth year working for CSE and O-level examinations, since the selection of pieces is representative of the various musical styles and forms studied. One or two commonly 'set' works are also included. Each piece is covered in units of 2-4 pages containing background information drawn from original sources, songs to sing with guitar accompaniments, notes on composers and their periods, suggestions for follow-up work, useful information about forms, styles, and instruments, numerous illustrations, and a quiz. A *Guide to the Music* with mainly single stave extracts is printed, so that the pupils can easily follow the main themes of each work as they listen.

In general, the pieces illustrate the theme that people, places and events have been a source of musical inspiration to many great composers: the character of Tam O'Shanter, the Vienna Woods, the Old Testament account of the creation of the world.

Resources required to make full use of *Portraits in Music* include recordings of all items listed on the Contents page. (A Discography is provided despite the fact that this, due to constant deletions, can prove more frustrating than helpful! The references are correct, to the best of our knowledge, at the time of going to press.) Scores of Bernstein's *West Side Story* and Smetana's *The Bartered Bride* may be borrowed from most public libraries and are necessary to provide piano accompaniments.

DAVID JENKINS
MARK VISOCCHI
1981

Tam O'Shanter

CONCERT OVERTURE

BY MALCOM ARNOLD (b. 1921)

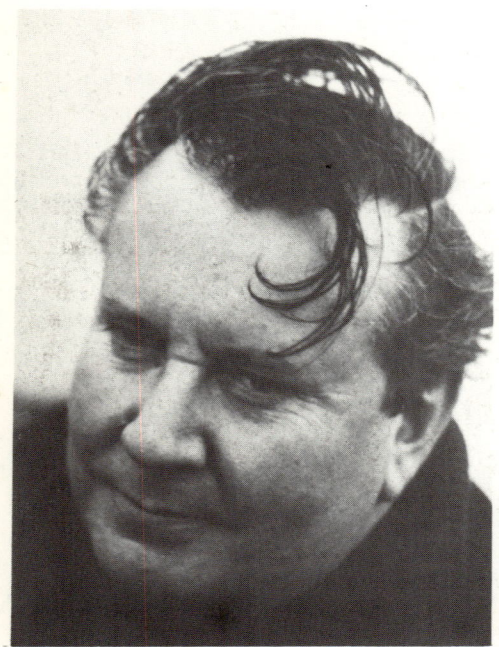

Malcolm Arnold was born at Northampton in 1921. At school he studied violin and trumpet, and when he was 17 he won a scholarship to the Royal College of Music. In 1941, after winning a prize for composition, he joined the London Philharmonic Orchestra as a trumpet player. After some years with the B.B.C. Symphony Orchestra he returned to the London Philharmonic Orchestra as first trumpet, all the time continuing to compose and attracting increased attention as a composer. A few years later he decided to devote himself full-time to composition. Among his music are choral works, concertos, symphonies, various orchestral pieces, chamber music, and music for films (including the score for *The Bridge on the River Kwai*).

Malcolm Arnold is known for his attractive melodies, full of character and a sense of fun, together with his imaginative use of woodwind, brass, and percussion instruments. All these can be heard in his concert overture *Tam O'Shanter* based on Robert Burns's poem of the same name.

Robert Burns, the poet who wrote 'Tam O'Shanter'

THE STORY

You will enjoy Malcom Arnold's *Tam O'Shanter* more if you read Burns's famous poem and become thoroughly familiar with the details of its story.

On the title page of his piece, Malcolm Arnold quotes the closing lines from Burns's cautionary tale:

Now, wha this tale o' truth shall read,
Ilk man, and mother's son, tak heed:
Whene'er to drink you are inclin'd,
Or cutty sarks run in your mind,
Think! ye may buy the joys o'er dear:
Remember Tam O'Shanter's meare.

Tam O'Shanter, 'a blethering, blustering, drunken blellum [babbler]', sets off home after a night's hard drinking. Outside the inn he mounts his mare, Meg, and boldly sets off into the stormy night with thunder and lightning accompanying him on his way. His journey home takes him past Kirk-Alloway, a sinister place notorious for murders, suicides, and accidents to lonely travellers. While Tam drunkenly sings to keep up his spirits he watches out 'lest bogles [hobgoblins] catch him unawares'.

As he approaches, Kirk-Alloway seems to be lit up and, through the sounds of the storm, Tam can hear the sound of bagpipes and merry-making. He urges his unwilling mare towards Kirk-Alloway to view the strangest sight he has ever seen:

Tam O'Shanter and his friends drinking at an inn

the Devil, in the shape of a shaggy black dog is playing the bagpipes while ugly warlocks and witches dance among the open coffins in the churchyard. Each corpse holds a candle to light up the altar where Tam sees on display, among other equally gruesome objects, bloodstained axes and murderers' bones.

As the dancing grows fast and furious, the old hags strip off their outer garments and dance in their 'sarks' (petticoats). Then Tam spots a comely young wench dressed in a 'cutty sark' (short petticoat) and as she dances in time with the fastest music played by Auld Nick (the Devil), Tam reacts over-excitedly and roars out 'Weel done, Cutty-sark!'.

Suddenly everything is plunged into darkness and, in a moment, Tam is riding from Kirk-Alloway hotly pursued by the 'hellish legion' led by Nannie, his girl in the cutty sark. In terror he rides on as fast as he can and just as the witches have almost caught up with him he reaches a running stream—which witches dare not cross. But just as Meg is jumping over the stream to safety, Nannie leaps at the mare, seizes her tail and pulls it off, leaving poor Meg with only a stump!

Tam O'Shanter crossing the stream on his horse, Meg, with Nannie in pursuit

Witches dancing among the coffins. In the left-hand corner, the Devil playing the bagpipes, in the centre the girl, Nannie, wearing her cutty sark

GUIDE TO THE MUSIC

The overture begins quietly with hushed strings, a drone on the clarinet and a very Scottish tune from the piccolo:

The mood is eerie and is interrupted by the timpani with rumblings of distant thunder; there is a storm brewing.

As Tam leaves the inn drunkenly 'crooning o'er some auld Scots sonnet', bassoons play a somewhat unsteady tune:

Tam mounts his disapproving mare (plaintive *glissandi* on trombones) and rides off into the night and the frightful storm (timpani and percussion). A terrifying crash from the orchestra marks the start of his homeward journey.

Tam rides on through thunder (*drums and cymbals*) and whistling wind (*piccolo and flute*). Now and then he can be heard above the storm bawling out (*trombone*) the auld Scots sonnet to help keep up his spirits and whipping his mare onwards through wind and rain.

Tam approaches the illuminated Kirk-Alloway and his curiosity overcomes his fear. He urges Meg up the path (*hesitant rising scale on brass*) and the music reaches a tremendous climax as the orchestra plays a lively bagpipe tune to accompany the witches' dancing:

The bagpipe tune alternates with a sort of jazzed-up hymn tune played by piccolos:

As attention focusses on the awful sights on the altar (*string trills and grisly brass chords*) the church bell tolls. The music gets wilder, the bell joins in the band, and the dissonant music shrieks on until the over-excited Tam cries out:

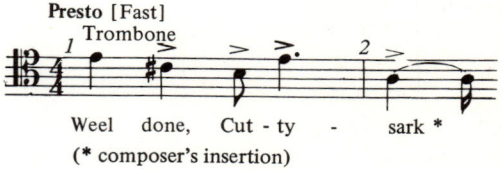

Immediately, the chase begins (*strings then woodwind playing up and down the scale and the brass joining in*). Tam gallops on but the witches gain on him (*orchestral passage repeated at rising pitch levels*). As they approach the stream the excitement is intense. Then Meg makes her leap to safety—but loses her tail (*cymbals clash*). The witches vanish (*upward sweep of clarinets*), the wind drops, and there is momentary peace . . .

before the overture ends with a final flurry and three resounding chords.

The Scottish highland bagpipe

Bagpipes are among the most ancient of musical instruments and date back to the Romans who had them in their armies. Today bagpipes can be found in most European countries. The instrument is of a different design in each country but always has a 'bag' which, when filled with air and squeezed, expels air which sounds the pipes. In the Northumbrian Bagpipe and the Scottish Lowland Bagpipe the bag is filled with air by a bellows held under the arm, while in the Scottish Highland Bagpipe the bag is filled with air from the player's mouth. Attached to the bag is the **chanter**, a pipe on which tunes are played. The chanter has either a single reed in its mouthpiece (like a clarinet) or a double reed (like an oboe). The reed produces the sound and different notes are made by the player by closing and opening holes in the tube with his fingers (like a recorder or any other woodwind instrument).

On most bagpipes there are also **drone pipes** which play all the time and are not touched by the player's fingers. The Highland Bagpipe normally has three drone pipes, two tenors and a bass, all tuned to the keynote (**A**). The bagpipe scale is the scale of A major with G natural instead of G sharp. Although some people find the drone and the rather harsh tone unattractive, Scots brought up to the sounds find the skirl of the pipes echoing across a valley from a distant hill exhilarating.

How the bagpipe works
A bag reservoir, inflated through a valve, supplies air to the fingered chanter and unfingered drone. The air vibrates the double reed of the chanter to produce a melody accompanied by a continuous hum or drone.

Wild landscape near Ben More, Scotland

FOLLOW UP

Malcom Arnold found inspiration in the work of Robert Burns on another occasion: the second of his *Scottish Dances* is based on Burns's song 'I'll ay ca' in by yon toon'. Learn to sing 'I'll ay ca' in by yon toon', then listen to how Malcolm Arnold 'dresses up' the tune in the second of his *Scottish Dances*.

Two movements from the Fantastic Symphony

BY HECTOR BERLIOZ (1803-1869)

Hector Berlioz was born near Grenoble, France. His father was a doctor. When he was old enough he went to Paris to take up medicine like his father, but soon abandoned his medical studies in favour of composing music. After studying at the Paris Conservatoire he aimed to win the much sought-after *Prix de Rome* so that he could compose without worries about money; he finally won the prize after four unsuccessful attempts!

Most of his life was spent in Paris where he mingled with French writers and painters, and he became the leading French composer of the Romantic period. His compositions for orchestra (besides the *Fantastic Symphony*) include the *Roman Carnival* overture and *Harold in Italy*, an orchestral piece with an important part for viola. He wrote choral music and operas, and was also a music critic.

As a composer he liked to use large forces of singers and instrumentalists, and this tendency was often caricatured in contemporary drawings.

In 1827 an English theatrical company visited Paris. Their repertory included *Hamlet* and *Romeo and Juliet*. Ophelia and Juliet were played by a young, beautiful, and talented Irish actress called Harriet Smithson. The combination of Shakespeare and Harriet overpowered the young composer Hector Berlioz. He fell in love with Shakespeare's Ophelia and Harriet Smithson; in a 'flash of lightning (she) illuminated the most remote depths of the heaven of art'. He could not sleep, work, or do anything, and roamed the streets of Paris summoning up sufficient strength to return to the theatre for 'another attack on my sensibilities'. He dropped with exhaustion wherever he happened to be, and on one occasion he alarmed the waiters at a cafe who thought he was dead.

In 1829 he still had not met Miss Smithson, although she was by this time aware of his passion for her. His feelings for her continued to haunt him, and in February 1830 he wanted to compose a new work which was to symbolise 'this infernal love of mine'. The musical ideas swam around in his head, but he found it impossible to commit his ideas to paper. In April he must have heard rumours about her doubtful respectability, since he wrote to his publisher saying that some 'horrible truths' had come to his attention, and had begun to cure him of his infatuation. It was Berlioz's infatuation for Harriet Smithson that formed the background to his *Fantastic Symphony*. Their romance subsequently followed a stormy path, but they were eventually married in 1833.

The French public in Berlioz's time was accustomed to large-scale concerts. Massive choral and orchestral forces were common, as were descriptive programme notes giving details about the musical works. For the first performance of the *Fantastic Symphony* (subtitled: 'Episode in the life of an artist') on 5 December 1830, Berlioz wrote the following programme note:

Portrait of Harriet Smithson, aged 19, who inspired Berlioz's 'Fantastic Symphony'

*A young musician of extraordinary sensibility and abundant imagination, in the depths of despair because of hopeless love, has poisoned himself with opium. The drug is too feeble to kill him but plunges him into a heavy sleep accompanied by weird visions. His sensations, emotions and memories, as they pass through his affected mind, are transformed into musical images and ideas. The beloved one herself becomes to him a melody, a recurrent theme (*idée fixe*) which haunts him continually.*

The **idée fixe**, literally 'fixed idea', in a musical context is a musical phrase or theme which occurs at intervals throughout the piece.

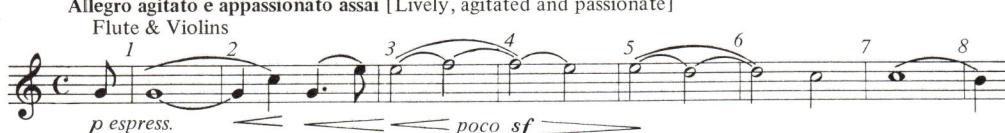

The *Fantastic Symphony* consists of five movements. Berlioz gave them the following titles: Reveries, Passions; A ball; In the country; March to the scaffold; Dream of a witches' sabbath.

We are going to look in detail at the second and fourth movements.

The clarinet

The clarinet is a member of the woodwind family and is about 66cm long. The sound is produced by the player blowing through a mouthpiece with a single reed attached. The reed is a piece of cane scraped flat. The highest notes on the clarinet sound rather shrill while the middle register is warm and expressive and the low register has a rich, hollow sound. Berlioz uses it in the last movement of the Fantastic Symphony.

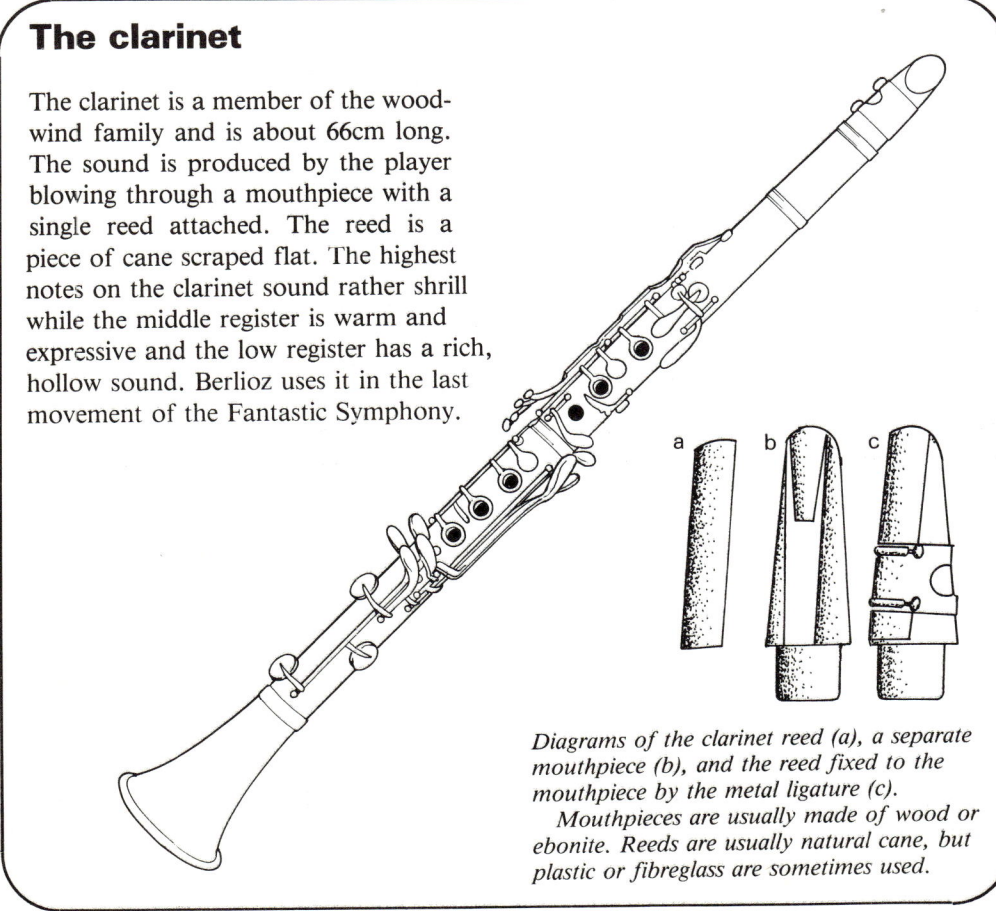

Diagrams of the clarinet reed (a), a separate mouthpiece (b), and the reed fixed to the mouthpiece by the metal ligature (c).

Mouthpieces are usually made of wood or ebonite. Reeds are usually natural cane, but plastic or fibreglass are sometimes used.

Waltzing at a ball in the 1840s

GUIDE TO THE MUSIC

SECOND MOVEMENT

A ball *Allegro non troppo*

At a ball, in the midst of a noisy, brilliant fête, the young man finds his beloved again.

The second movement is a waltz—an unusual movement to find in a symphony, although the use of a dance movement was common in the symphonies of Haydn and Mozart.

The romance of the ballroom—glittering chandeliers, the ladies in elegant long dresses, the gentlemen in military or evening finery—is conjured up in a cascade of harps and strings which introduce the flowing waltz tune.

The waltz, played sweetly and tenderly, has a Viennese swing to it, and it is no surprise to find that Berlioz later became a keen follower of the music of Johann Strauss.

The *idée fixe* returns transformed into waltz-time. But the scoring has none of the simplicity of its first appearance, perhaps suggesting a face recognised at a distance across a crowded ballroom.

As the dance continues the *idée fixe* is absorbed into the music of the waltz and the mood gradually becomes more and more lively. Just before it is overshadowed by the final flourish of the waltz the *idée fixe* returns a second time, now isolated and pleading.

FOURTH MOVEMENT

March to the scaffold   *Allegretto non troppo*

The young man dreams he has killed his loved one, that he is condemned to death and led to his execution. A march, now gloomy and ferocious, now solemn and brilliant, accompanies the procession. Noisy outbursts are followed without pause by the heavy sound of footsteps. Finally, like a last thought of love, the *idée fixe* appears for a moment, to be cut off by the fall of the axe.

The last two movements of the *Fantastic Symphony* are the most obviously theatrical of the piece, although a 'March to the scaffold' would not have been difficult for Berlioz's first audience to imagine, bearing in mind recent political events of the French Revolution.

The *March to the scaffold* opens with a suggestion of the tread of heavy footsteps:

The second march tune is full of aggressive splendour:

The remainder of the movement consists of continued reference to these two themes. The orchestral build-up suddenly halts—a shrill clarinet records a final memory of the beloved, cut short by a sudden orchestral *fortissimo* chord marking the fall of the axe.

For those enthralled by the gory details one can actually hear the severed head tumble unceremoniously into the waiting basket!

The guillotine claims nine victims

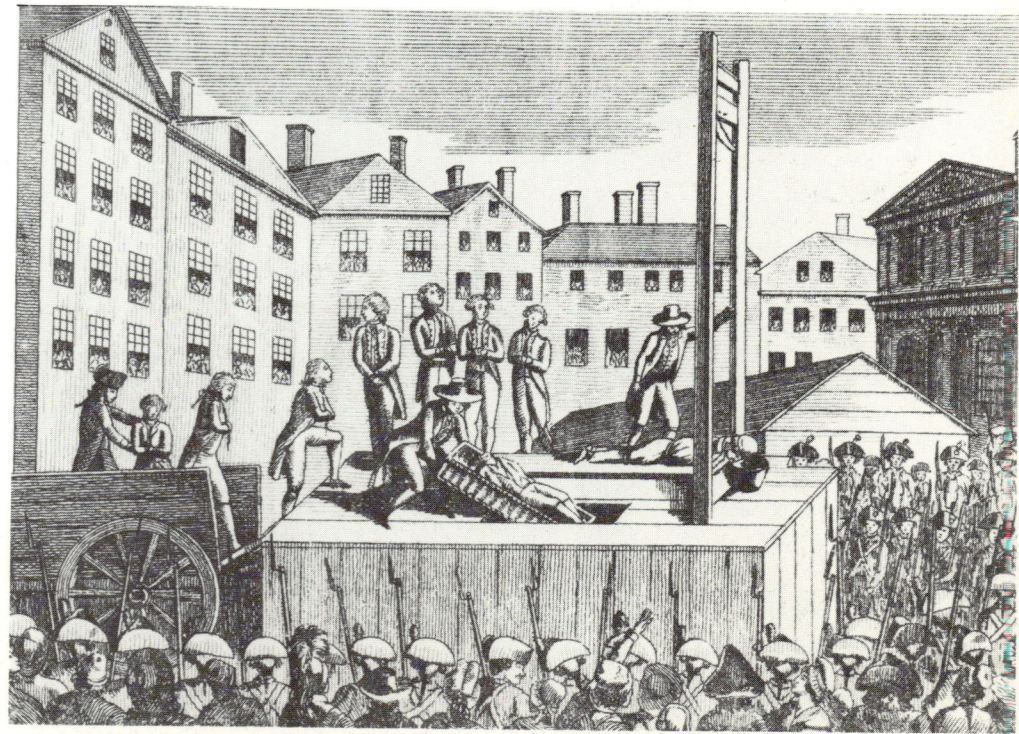

Romanticism in music

The music of Berlioz illustrates a number of characteristics which were typical of early 19th-century music.

1. Rebellion and revolution against oppression; the fourth movement of the *Fantastic Symphony* ('March to the scaffold') pictures the hero willing to die for his beliefs.
2. The dignity and worthiness of man as an individual—his thoughts and feelings. The first movement of the *Fantastic Symphony* (Reveries, Passions) concerns the emotional state of the young man.
3. Love of various kinds;
   (a) Love of all mankind.
   (b) Ideal and eternal love; the *idée fixe*, which appears in one form or another in all five movements of the *Fantastic Symphony*, represents 'the beloved one'.
   (c) Young love and its heart-aches; the tenderness and romance of the Waltz (second) movement portrays this.
   (d) Love of nature; the third movement, *Ranz des Vaches* ('cowherd's call') is a typical natural scene—cowherd's piping, the roll of distant thunder, and so on.
4. Interest in the mysterious and supernatural; the fifth movement, *Witches' Sabbath*, combines a grotesque version of the *idée fixe* with the *Dies Irae* melody from the Requiem for the Dead.

Pastoral scene by the 19th-century French painter Corot

These characteristics make up what is known as *Romanticism* in music (and in the arts generally). Two sets of historical circumstances were largely responsible for the Romantic movement:

1. The political and social upheavals which began with the French Revolution of 1789 and were followed in the first half of the 19th century by a series of revolutions which eventually brought down the monarchies of Europe.
2. The economic changes brought about by 'The Industrial Revolution' which was taking place in Britain, France, Prussia, and Austria.

These 'revolutions' created a mood of change. They gave birth to a new class of people whose wealth was based on commerce and industry, and whose tastes were different from the aristocracy of the 18th century.

New tastes led to changes in the way symphonies were written. They now had:

1. longer movements
2. bolder harmonies
3. a link with literary/pictorial ideas
4. larger orchestral forces
5. more dramatic content
   (a) dynamic contrast (extremes of louds and softs)
   (b) thematic contrast
   (c) instrumental contrast

FOLLOW UP

1. Using our discussion of the characteristics of Romantic music as a starting point, listen to the other movements of Berlioz's *Fantastic Symphony* and see how many of the characteristics of Romantic music you can trace.

2. Berlioz has provided us with some fascinating insights into the French musical scene of his day through his writings in such books as *Evening with the Orchestra* and his *Memoirs*. Read about one of the pranks they got up to in the orchestral pit!

Adagio from SPARTACUS

BY ARAM KHACHATURIAN (1903-1978)

Aram Khachaturian with the composer Dmitri Shostakovich's son Maxim

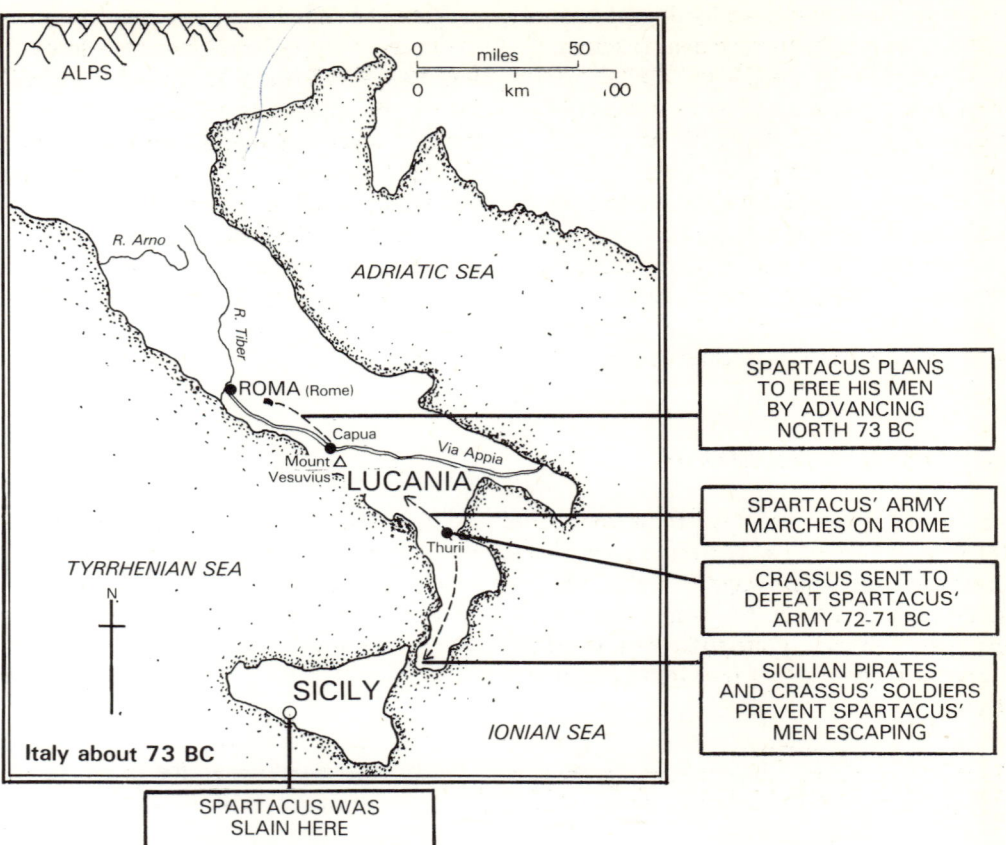

Aram Ilyich Khachaturian was born into an Armenian family in Tibilisi (Tiflis) in Georgia, Russia, on 6 June 1903. As a youngster, he received no formal music education although he did manage to play bass parts by ear on the tuba in his school band. When he was 19 he went to Moscow. There, despite the fact that he could neither read music nor speak Russian, he enrolled as a student of cello and composition at a city music school and, later, at the Moscow Conservatory. He left the conservatory in 1934, the year of the first performance of his first symphony. By this time he also had written military marches, chamber music, pieces for piano, and various orchestral works. In 1939, he was awarded the Order of Lenin and, a year later, won the Stalin Prize for his violin concerto. He wrote his second symphony for the twenty-fifth anniversary of the October Revolution. Among his other compositions are choral pieces, film and ballet music, and a series of patriotic songs for the Red Army.

THE STORY OF SPARTACUS

Spartacus was the leader in the Gladiatorial War against Rome in the years 73-71 B.C. He was born in Thrace, Greece. Captured by the Romans, he was sold as a slave and taken to Capua to be trained as a gladiator. In 73 B.C., with 70 comrades, he escaped from Capua and took refuge on Mount Vesuvius where he was joined by other fugitives. His army grew in number and soon was strong enough to inflict two defeats on forces from Rome. He declared the abolition of slavery and with his victorious army, now about one hundred thousand strong, he advanced northwards towards the Alps. His plan was to lead his men out of Italy, disband them and allow them to return home free. But his army, encouraged by their successes, insisted Spartacus lead them against Rome. He billeted his army for the winter of 72-71 B.C. at Thurii, Lucania, where the Roman Commander, Licinius Crassus, was sent to defeat him. Spartacus's army managed to break through the Roman lines and began to march towards Rome. But Crassus caught up with him and, with Spartacus's army quarrelling among themselves and consequently divided, Crassus defeated most of them easily and then went in pursuit of Spartacus himself. While trying to cross into Sicily, Spartacus was betrayed by Sicilian pirates and many of his soldiers were taken prisoner by Crassus. Spartacus and his army were finally defeated at a battle which took place at the river Silarus. Spartacus himself was slain. Many slaves who escaped northwards were killed by Roman legions led by another Roman general, Pompey, and six thousand survivors were crucified, by Crassus, along the Appian Way.

Ever since, Spartacus has been regarded as the patron saint of revolutionaries.

However, his role was really that of a crusader in a fight for personal freedom.

A visit to Italy in 1950 was the inspiration for Khachaturian's music for his ballet *Spartacus*. The ballet is essentially a narrative ballet (that is, a ballet with a story) in the classic-romantic tradition. As you would expect, it contains set dances which digress from the main line of the plot. The principal characters of the ballet are Spartacus, his wife Phrygia, the tyrant Crassus and his mistress Aegina.

On the night before Spartacus's last battle (Act 3, Scene 3 of the ballet), while his encamped soldiers are asleep, after a night of revelry, Spartacus unsuccessfully attempts to comfort Phrygia. She is afraid of the fate which awaits her husband on the battlefield. Together they dance an *Adagio* which is accompanied by 'love' music that has topped the pop music charts.

GUIDE TO THE MUSIC

The piece begins with a lengthy introduction. The first section sets a menacing mood through the use of low, repeated harp sounds, rather 'tipsy' bassoons and muted horn calls. Dotted rhythms suggest the marching of soldiers in the background. The second section of the introduction sets a more optimistic mood; the strings enter with more expressive phrases. Flute trills warn us of the entry of the 'love' theme of Spartacus and Phrygia, played at first quietly on the oboe.

Theme A

The string section takes over the 'love' theme and gives it a lush scoring, building to a climax.

Suddenly the mood changes with drooping, expressive string phrases, perhaps suggesting Phrygia's foreboding of the death of Spartacus. As in the first section of the introduction, menacing repeated notes in the bass over which the harmony changes produce a feeling of tension.

Theme B

Gradually the more optimistic tone returns with brief fanfares on the horns and trumpets. The pace of the music increases and its volume builds up to usher in a return of the 'love' theme played even more richly by the strings. Above them rise trumpet fanfares. The *ff* lush scoring gradually dies away and a quieter, more reflective version of the theme is again heard on strings. A solo violin, accompanied by string tremolos, brings the piece to a hushed close.

Two stills from the film 'Spartacus' starring Kirk Douglas: Spartacus rides into battle and (inset) Spartacus with his wife (played by Jean Simmons)

FOLLOW UP

1. Khachaturian has an uncanny though unintentional knack of getting his tunes into the hit parade. Listen to his 'Sabre Dance' and 'The Dance of the Young Maidens' from his ballet *Gayaneh*.

2. Find out the names of other great Russian ballets in the classic-romantic tradition. Try to listen to some music from them.

THE STARS & STRIPES FOREVER

MARCH

BY JOHN PHILIP SOUSA (1854-1932)

Brass bands came into being around 150 years ago. The first brass band was the Blackdyke Mills Band which began as a reed band (i.e. a mixture of woodwind instruments) and later added brass instruments. Brass bands became more popular as improvements were made to existing instruments and as new ones were invented during the 19th century. Until that time, reed instruments dominated town, military, and court bands and the standard band of the 18th century consisted of eight instruments arranged in pairs—two flutes, two oboes, two bassoons, and two horns. Mozart, Haydn, and Beethoven wrote music for groups of instruments like these.

The earliest British brass band contests limited band numbers to 12. Even today bands usually consist of no more than 24 players. Limiting the number of players in a band makes each member think of himself as a soloist, every note he plays being vitally important to the performance. Brass bands are rather like small chamber orchestras. The military band (which includes reed instruments as well as brass instruments) is a larger and more powerful combination. This is because it has to play in the open air and all soldiers must be able to hear the music when they are marching on parade.

In recent times brass band music has developed tremendously. Not only are there special brass band arrangements of popular music (excerpts from operas, overtures, etc.) by composers of the last 150 years or so, but also modern music has been specially written for brass bands, by Malcolm Arnold and others. An interest has also developed in playing music of the 16th and 17th centuries. Competitions encourage friendly rivalry between different bands and so the standard of playing is continually improving.

Poster advertising a performance by Sousa and his band

SOUSA'S LIFE

'A march should make a man with a wooden leg step out'.
So said John Philip Sousa, the most famous military bandmaster who ever lived. Sousa was born in Washington on 6 November 1854. His father was a Portuguese immigrant who played the trombone in the U.S. Marine Band. As a young boy, John Philip Sousa was able to attend the rehearsals and concerts of the

Marine Band. He knew all the players and became familiar with the music they played. Occasionally he was allowed to join in playing a simple percussion part—perhaps for the triangle or the cymbals. As a child, he learned to play the violin, and when he grew up he became leader of an orchestra in Washington. In 1880, he was appointed conductor of the U.S. Marine Band and wrote many of his famous marches for this band. 12 years later he formed his own band and took it on a world tour during which he wrote more than 50 marches and 7 comic operas! He went on travelling for about 20 years. He died in Reading, Pennsylvania, on 6 March 1932.

Sousa's band
Sousa's touring concert band had 49 players. It consisted mainly of reed instruments—25 altogether, including oboes, clarinets, bassoons, and saxophones: his 19 brass instruments consisted of cornets, horns, trumpets, trombones, euphoniums, and tubas. To complete the band of 49 members, Sousa added two flutes and three percussion players.

Sousa's beard
Sousa's appearance on the rostrum was very smart and impressive. Not very tall, he had a bushy beard and a moustache. At that time, when Sousa was quite young, most of the better musicians in America were foreigners. American musicians, usually clean-shaven, were not taken seriously; nor was their music considered to be of much worth. So that people would take him seriously, Sousa grew a beard and moustache to make him look like a foreigner—and his plan succeeded. People *did* take him and his music seriously. At last, he decided to get rid of his beard and, to the surprise of his audience and especially his wife, he suddenly shaved it off in the middle of a concert!

Sousa's travels
During his famous touring years, Sousa calculated that he and his concert band travelled about one and a quarter million miles by land or sea. The tours began on 6 November 1910, his fifty-sixth birthday. One of his visits was to Wales where the band gave a concert in the drill hall at Merthyr Tydfil. The stage had to be specially enlarged to accommodate Sousa's band and the stage extension was a very frail-looking construction. During the concert, the stage extension collapsed and down went Sousa, rostrum, music and a number of band members. In the turmoil, Sousa temporarily lost his glasses; but the concert continued with half of the band on stage and the other half where the stage extension *had* been. Later it was discovered that the contractor who built the stage extension was both a carpenter *and* an undertaker!

There are many amusing stories about Sousa, and he himself had a tremendous sense of humour. Being a famous personality, he was always being recognised. Once, however, at a railway station, he was asked by a lady, 'Are you the conductor?' Sousa replied 'Yes, I am the conductor'. The lady asked 'Can you tell me if the 9.30 train has left?' Sousa said 'No'. 'A fine conductor *you* are!' she exclaimed. Sousa explained that he was 'the conductor of a brass band, not a railroad train!'

Sousa at the White House
In 1865, at the end of the American Civil War, Sousa was 11 years old. As he stood outside the White House with his parents and family, flag in hand, cheering the President, Andrew Jackson, who was reviewing his victorious troops, little did he think as he stood there, fascinated by the music of the bands marching past, that one day he himself would play at the White House.

When he was appointed conductor of the U.S. Marine Band, his duties included providing music at the White House, outdoors to accompany state occasions, and indoors at dinners or receptions. Sousa was very popular with a number of American Presidents. They were impressed by Sousa's careful planning of music programmes for these occasions. For the first and most important guests Sousa's band played quietly and without percussion allowing the President to exchange greetings in a quiet and dignified manner. With the arrival of guests who were less important the band played gradually louder and quicker numbers. This made the guests move more quickly and prevented them from indulging in long conversations. The President was grateful for Sousa's help and declared that his bandmaster had made it possible for him to get through all his introductions in double quick time!

Sousa (centre) as conductor of the US Marine Band in 1890

Some brass band instruments

The euphonium and the horn family

An instrument which looks and sounds like a small tuba, the mellow-toned **euphonium** is the principal middle-range soloist in the brass band. A number of different instruments of the euphonium type appear in the brass band. They are often referred to as 'horns' though they are not related to the French Horn and do not even look like that instrument. **Tenor** and **baritone horns** are much the same size as the euphonium. **Bass horns**—sometimes called saxhorns after their inventor Adolphe Saxe—are made in several different pitch sizes.

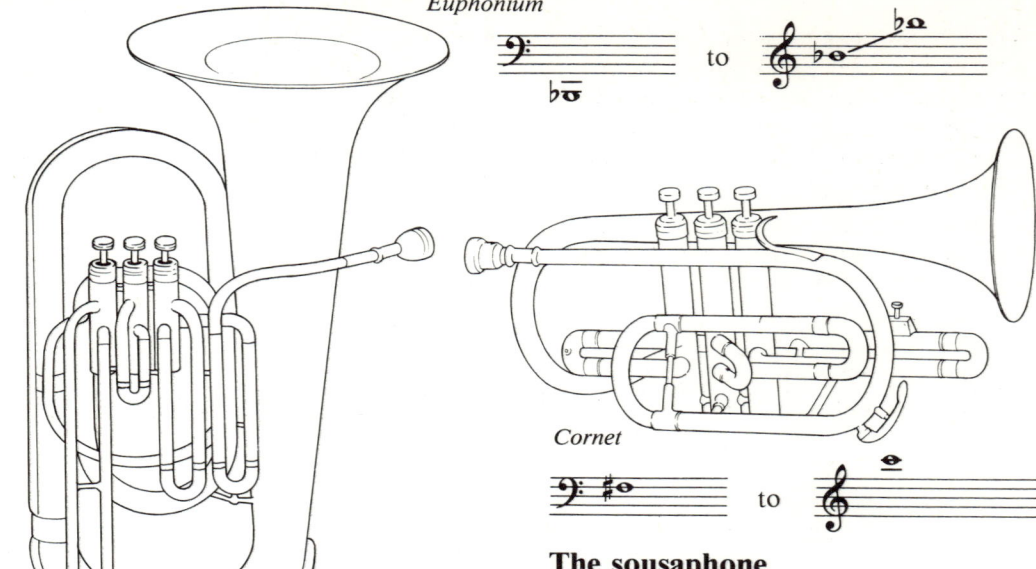

Euphonium

Cornet

The sousaphone

The largest and deepest-sounding instruments of the brass band include the **tuba**, the **bombardon**, the **helicon** and the **sousaphone**. The helicon is an instrument which, when played, looks as if it had wound itself round the player. The sousaphone (invented by Sousa himself) is a modified helicon. Sousa altered the design of the instrument, enlarging the bell and making it detachable—in fact, the bell is over 60cm in diameter and is perched above the player's head, so it has to be securely fixed! The sousaphone became a very popular instrument not only in military bands but also in jazz bands.

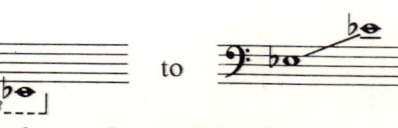

Euphonium, sousaphone and cornet being played

The cornet

Though it looks like a trumpet its tone is sweeter and softer. Differences in design account for their tonal differences: the brass tube of the cornet is conical (like a trombone). The mouthpieces of the instruments also are shaped differently.

Sousaphone

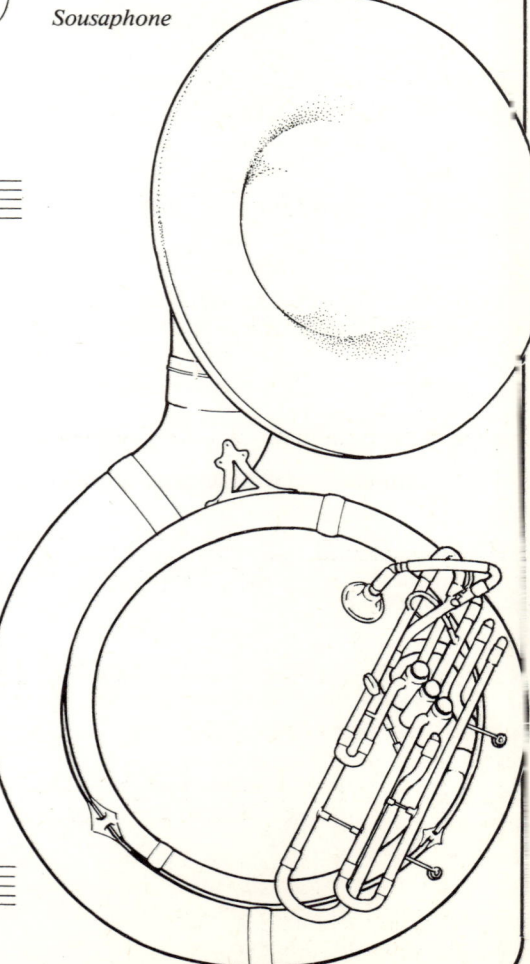

GUIDE TO THE MUSIC

The Stars and Stripes Forever, composed in 1897, is Sousa's most famous march. The music came to him when he was returning to America by ocean liner from a tour in Italy. This popular march is generally regarded as an expression of American patriotism and rivals the country's national anthem in popularity, rather like Britain's 'Land of Hope and Glory'. Sousa set words to the Trio (middle section) of the piece, beginning 'Hurrah for the flag of the free'. This arrangement is widely used in American schools on special occasions.

The music of *The Stars and Stripes Forever* is organised to Sousa's favourite plan: following an impressive introduction, there appears a sprightly first tune (**A**).

followed by a broader melody (**B**)

which leads to the famous Trio theme (**C**)

The Trio is interrupted by a highly-spirited section (**D**)

but returns finally in a tremendous climax with piccolo and other decorations providing new instrumental colours.

Sousa's musical form could be summarised thus: **A B C D C D C**.

Here are the main tunes of another of Sousa's famous marches *Semper fidelis*. Listen to this piece and pick out the tunes below as you listen.

How does the musical form of this march compare with that used in *The Stars and Stripes Forever?*

PACIFIC 231

TONE POEM

BY ARTHUR HONEGGER (1892-1955)

Honegger on the footplate of a LNER train in March 1927. He was then in London for a performance of 'Pacific 231' at the Albert Hall.

Arthur Honegger was born at Le Havre, in France, in March 1892. His parents were Swiss. He studied music in Zürich and Paris and his first important pieces appeared in 1916. Among his compositions are operas, ballets, incidental music for plays, radio, and films, choral and orchestral works, chamber music, and songs. The only piece of music by Honegger that has achieved anything like general popularity is his tone poem *Pacific 231*.

When Honegger was a small boy one of his favourite pastimes was train-spotting at Le Havre, where he lived. As he grew up his interest in trains remained, and he kept two miniature models of railway engines on the desk of the studio where he worked when he moved to Paris. It was not surprising that his passion for trains led him to compose a piece about them. Here is an extract from an interview with Honegger in which the composer gives his own account of the music of *Pacific 231*:

I have always had a passionate liking for locomotives; for me they are living things, and I love them as others love women or horses. What I have endeavoured to describe in Pacific 231 is not an imitation of the sounds of the locomotive, but the translation into musical terms of the visual impression and the physical sensation of it. It shows the objective contemplation: the tranquil breathing of the machine in repose, the effort to start, the progressive gathering speed, leading from the lyric state to the pathetic, of a train of 300 tons hurling itself through the night at 120 miles an hour.

For my subject I have chosen the locomotive type 'Pacific 231', for heavy trains of great speed.

He was 31 years old when he wrote *Pacific 231*, and he spent most of 1923 working on it although the piece itself only lasts about six minutes!

GUIDE TO THE MUSIC

As you listen to the piece look out for four main sections.

1   At the beginning we hear the intermittent hissing of steam from the engine as it stands at rest. Gradually, the engine moves off and gains speed; the music here is arranged in short bursts of different 'textures', each one gaining in speed, activity, and force to represent the massive locomotive gathering momentum.

Theme B

2 Once under way, the music settles down into a rhythmic swaying motion and swift-moving tunes criss-cross one another like railway lines merging in front of the speeding train.

Theme C

3 After this more melodic section, the music subsides for the moment and a new sense of building up to a climax of speed and noise is established. Here are the three elements to listen for:
(a) a lot of 'surface' activity in the music suggesting the moving mechanical parts of the train.
(b) a sustained tune on horns suggesting the engine's massive power.

Theme D

(c) a reference to the criss-crossing tune of section (b).

The climax builds up as trumpets take over the sustained tune from the horns and the music rises in pitch and volume. We have a clear picture of Honegger's 'train of 300 tons hurling itself through the night at 120 miles an hour'.

4 Suddenly the brakes are applied as the train approaches its destination. All the surface activity in the music gradually slows down to match and eventually comes to rest, as does *Pacific 231*.

QUOTES FROM THE CRITICS

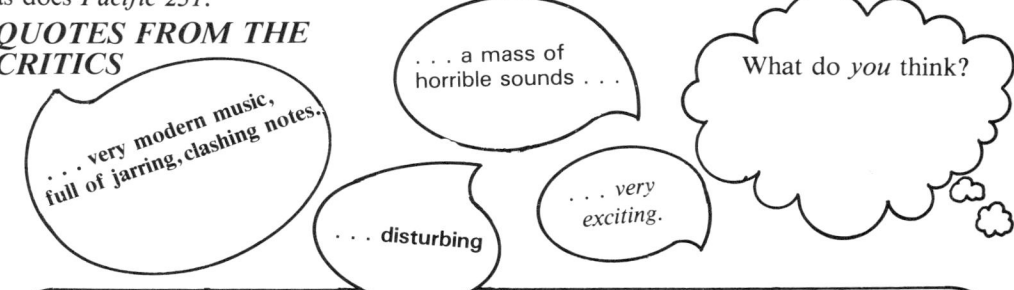

Dissonance

Play the following chords on the piano or tuned percussion.

Now play the following on the piano or tuned percussion.

The first set of chords were pleasant-sounding and are what we call musical **consonances**; the next set you would probably agree are much less pleasant and set up tensions in our ears which we call **dissonances**.

The use of consonances and dissonances by composers has varied during the course of musical history. But there is one unchanging 'law' about dissonances which is related to the laws of physics—dissonances are most effective when they are 'set off' by consonances, so the normal pattern for composers to use is:

Consonance ⟶ Dissonance ⟶ Consonance

Listen to the following example:

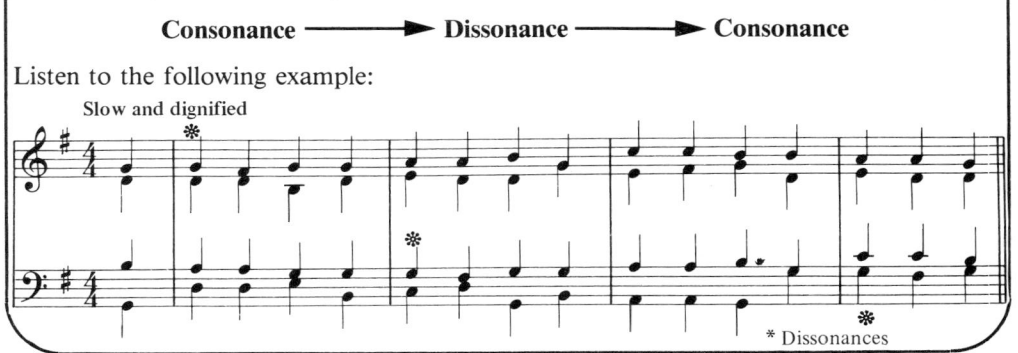

* Dissonances

FOLLOW UP

Letters of thanks, letters from banks,
Letters of joy from girl and boy,
Receipted bills and invitations
To inspect new stock or to visit relations,
And applications for situations,
And timid lovers' declarations,
And gossip, gossip from all the nations,
News circumstantial, news financial,
Letters with holiday snaps to enlarge in,
Letters with faces scrawled on the margin,
Letters from uncles, cousins and aunts,
Letters to Scotland from the South of France,
Letters of condolence to Highlands and Lowlands,
Written on paper of every hue,
The pink, the violet, the white and the blue,
The chatty, the catty, the boring, the adoring,
The cold and official and the heart's outpouring,
Clever, stupid, short and long,
The typed and the printed and the spelt all wrong.

(extract from *Night Mail* by W. H. Auden)

Try to make up some background music for a reading of Auden's poem *Night Mail*. Make up your piece using some of the ideas below:

1. Use some of these word patterns to make a picture in sound of railway noises.

SOUNDS	IDEAS
Diddle-ee-dee, diddle-ee-dum Biddle-ee-dee, biddle-ee-da	Train on the open track
Diddle-clank-clatter-bang, clatter-batter-bonk	Train going over the points
Oinch, groinch, squeak, squerk	Waggons grinding on the rails
Blam-blam-blam-blam	Train going through the station

2. Use untuned percussion instruments playing *ostinati* (repeated patterns) to make railway noises and rhythms.

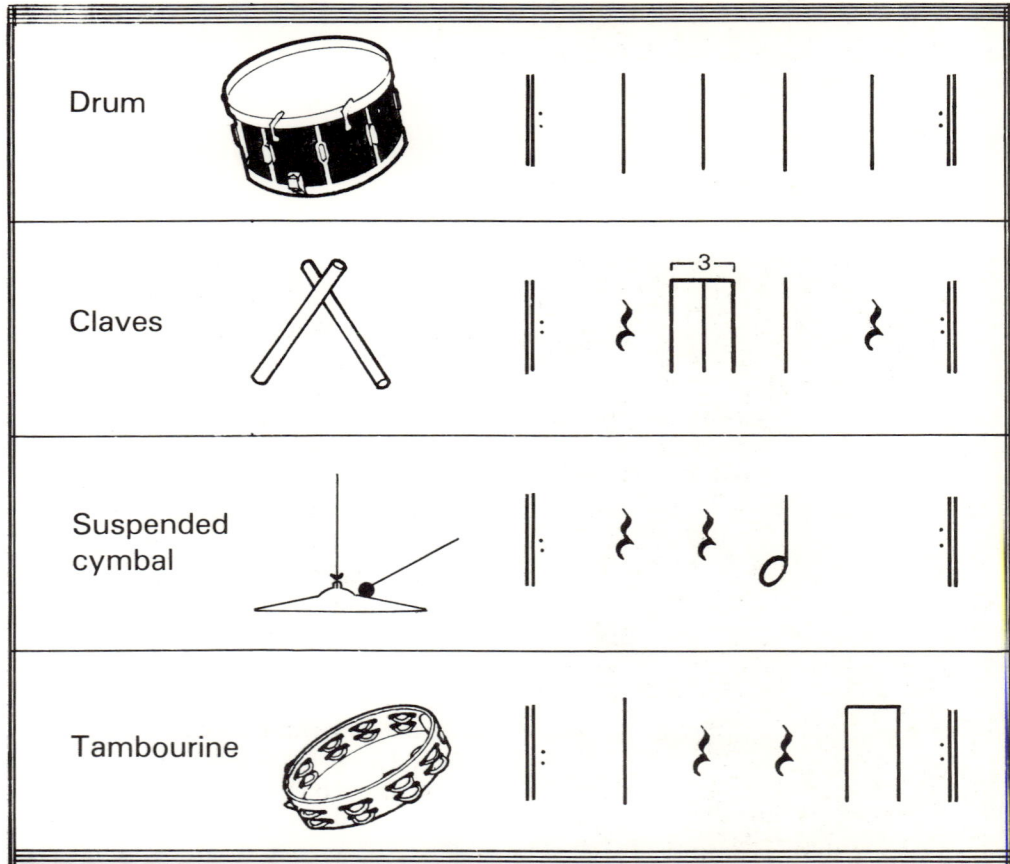

In composing your music think of the following points:

(a) Its structure; do you want to follow closely the sense of the poem or just provide a general railway-noise background?

(b) Elements of contrast; think about contrasts of speed, dynamics (louds and softs), material which might be effective and appropriate.

(c) How to organise your performance; do you want to write out a 'score' or a set of instructions for performers (you will need to think out how to notate the effects you want) or do you want your piece to be composer-directed?

Your teacher will help you to discuss and decide on these possibilities.

Tape record your music and use it to accompany a 'live' reading of Auden's poem.

Orchestral prelude from
The Creation

ORATORIO

BY JOSEPH HAYDN (1732-1809)

Haydn's birthplace at Rohrau, Austria.

Joseph Haydn was born at Rohrau, in Austria, in 1732, in a small cottage built by his father who was a wheelwright. Haydn's father loved music, had a pleasant tenor voice, and often accompanied his singing on the harp. At the end of the day's work the family often sat down to make music together. Haydn's musical gifts were evident from an early age. When he was eight years old he was offered a place in the Cathedral Choir-school in Vienna where he was taught to play harpsichord and violin while at the same time receiving a good general education. Even at this early age Haydn knew what he wanted to do in music—he wanted to be a composer.

In his teens he left the choir-school and earned a poor living as a music teacher in Vienna. Luck came his way in 1759 when he was appointed conductor of the orchestra of a nobleman. Then, two years later, the powerful Prince Esterházy offered him a post which put him in charge of the orchestra, church music, and operas at his country castle at Eisenstadt, and Haydn remained in the employment of the Esterházy family until 1790. Here he composed symphonies, concertos, string quartets, choral works, and other music which made his name famous throughout Europe. In 1791 and 1794 he was invited to come to London to take part in public concerts, and Oxford University conferred on him the honorary degree of Doctor of Music. In 1795 he settled down in Vienna and lived there for the remainder of his life honoured by everyone from the Emperor downwards. He died there in 1809, aged 77.

Joseph Haydn was a cheerful and genial personality and these personal qualities are reflected in his music which is highly tuneful and often light-hearted. Music of this type abounds in his famous oratorio, *The Creation*, composed in 1797-98.

Esterházy in 1766, where Haydn spent the greater part of each year. It stands in lonely, marshy countryside, originally part of Austria, now Hungary.

Oratorio

Oratorio originated about 1600 in performances at the Oratory (chapel) of St. Philip Neri in Rome, hence the name. Oratorios consist of lengthy musical settings of religious words set out in dramatic form—rather like an opera without costumes or scenery. In fact, in Haydn's time they were sometimes performed in a theatre. Since 1600 many composers have written oratorios. Well-known examples are Handel's *Messiah*, Mendelssohn's *Elijah* and Elgar's *The Dream of Gerontius*.

GUIDE TO THE MUSIC

Haydn's oratorio begins with a representation of Chaos which preceded the creation of the world. The opening of this orchestral prelude is a mighty sound, played in unison (i.e. the whole orchestra plays the same note).

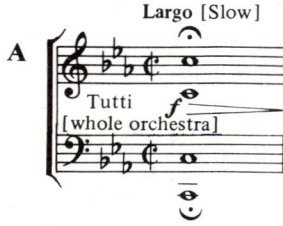

This perhaps represents the vastness and emptiness of space. What now follows would appear to be the beginnings of the creation of the world:

You will notice that in bar 4, where the orchestra plays loudly for the second time, the opening unison has gathered other notes—something is beginning to form in the wilderness of space. In musical terms, order slowly emerges as the key of C minor becomes established. The music then drifts towards a new key a related one with the same key signature, the major key of E flat. This in musical terms perhaps represents 'a natural gravitational movement'. (Haydn was a friend of the great astronomer, Herschel, and also was very knowledgeable about the scientific thinking of his day.) In bar 21 we find ourselves violently pulled into a new, and this time unrelated, key—D flat:

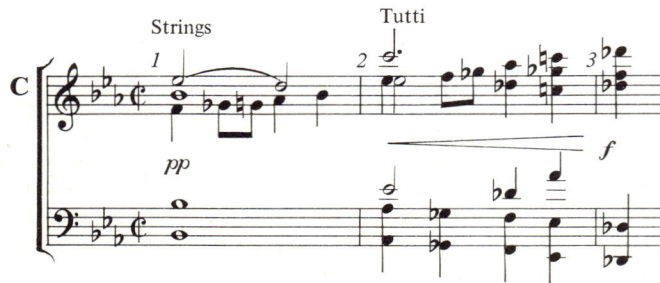

Haydn crossing to England during a storm, an unforgettable experience which he drew upon in a later part of the music in 'The Creation'

At this point a short melody emerges . . .

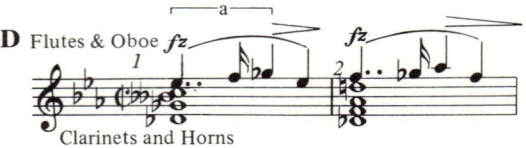

which, within a few bars, re-establishes the key of E flat and forms the basis of the melody which follows. For a while, order seems established as we remain in this key.

However, Chaos soon returns to the universe. Haydn gradually goes back to his original key of C minor and the short figure (a) from (**D**), played by various orchestral instruments, is present throughout this passage. The unison C, heard at the start of the piece as a sustained note, now returns in thunderous repeated notes . . .

and is followed by a modified version of the opening music. There is a further reference to figure (a) from (**D**). The music now drifts towards its conclusion but even here the short figure remains with us.

Haydn's vision of Chaos ends quietly in the darkness of low-pitched C minor chords.

Poster for the first performance of 'The Creation'

Haydn playing in a string quartet

The old Court Theatre, Vienna, around 1809, the year of Haydn's death

FOLLOW UP

'His Highness expects Mr Haydn to behave as an honourable officer of a princely establishment. To wit: to be always sober, to behave not rudely but politely and with consideration towards the musicians under his direction, and to be modest, quiet and honest in his conduct. Whenever there is music for His Highness, Mr Haydn will be responsible not only for his own but for his musicians' becoming appearance in proper livery, according to instructions with white stockings, white linen, well powdered, and either with pigtails or with hair-bags, but all in the same attire . . .

'Mr Haydn will write at the order of His Highness such music as may be commanded; and he will make no communication of such music to others, still less have it copied for anybody else, keeping it solely at the disposition of His Highness; nor will he write for anybody else without His gracious permission . . .

'Mr Haydn will appear every day, both in the morning and in the afternoon, in the "Antichambre", to receive his orders for the day regarding the music. And having done so, he will communicate them to his musicians and make sure that they arrive punctually according to order . . .

'It is his duty to take care of all the instruments with the utmost conscientiousness, lest they be damaged or made unusable, and he will be responsible for same. He will duly instruct the singers, lest they forget in the country what they have learned in Vienna, with much work and expense, from distinguished masters.'

This quotation is from the written instructions concerning Haydn's duties as master of the music of Prince Esterházy at Eisenstadt. It provides us with an insight into the conditions under which a musician in the 18th century had to live and work. Compare Haydn's way of life with how musicians earn their living today.

Serenade from
Don Giovanni

OPERA

BY WOLFGANG AMADEUS MOZART (1756-1791)

Wolfgang Amadeus Mozart was born in Salzburg, Austria, in 1756. His father was a fine violinist and a member of the Court Orchestra of the Archbishop of Salzburg. When Wolfgang was only four years old he began to learn to play the harpsichord and also to compose music. When his sister Anna Maria was aged ten and Wolfgang six their father decided that they had made sufficient progress in music to be brought before the public. So the Mozart family began a European tour, giving recitals in Munich, Vienna, Paris, and before the Court at Versailles. In London, the talented children played for King George III and also appeared in public concerts. Further travels took them to Holland, Switzerland, and to Italy where the Pope conferred a knighthood on the young lad of 13. Throughout this period his father was also teaching him composition. The young Mozart composed incessantly. He wrote his first symphony at the age of eight, his first oratorio at the age of 12 and his first opera, performed in Salzburg, at the age of 13. The elderly Archbishop of Salzburg always treated Mozart with great kindness and gave him a musical position at Court. But when the Archbishop died his successor was much less interested in Mozart and his family and, at the age of 25, Mozart resigned and left Salzburg for Vienna. Here he married, and despite a minor position given him by the Austrian Emperor, he was quite poor. His music, however, enjoyed great success: operas, symphonies, concertos, chamber music, piano music, choral music—all poured from his pen. No-one ever composed more easily, quickly, or effortlessly than Mozart. Tragically, he died in Vienna in 1791 at the age of only 35, of uraemia (kidney failure). This great musical genius was so poor that when he died he was buried in a pauper's grave.

Mozart's great opera *Don Giovanni* was composed in 1787. When Mozart composed this opera he put off writing the overture, and the day before the first performance of the opera it was still not written! That night, while his wife read to him to keep him awake, he composed the overture. After that, the different orchestral parts had to be copied out (a long and laborious business) so that there was no time to rehearse the overture. At that first performance of the opera, the orchestra actually played the overture at sight!

Don Giovanni invites the Commendatore to dinner

Don Giovanni (the Italian form of Don Juan) is the main character of Mozart's opera. He has a greedy eye for the ladies and in the opera begins his adventures with Donna Anna who rejects his advances. Her father, the Commendatore, is killed defending his daughter's honour in a duel with Don Giovanni. The bold seducer goes on to pursue one girl after another. Finally, taking refuge in a cemetery, he finds a statue of the Commendatore and mockingly invites the statue to dine with him. The statue, to Don Giovanni's astonishment, nods its head and accepts the invitation. On arrival at Don Giovanni's house it reprimands its host for all his past misdeeds. Devils appear from below and take Don Giovanni off to his well-deserved punishment in hell.

In Act 2, Scene 1, Don Giovanni, disguised as a manservant, serenades a young peasant girl who has attracted his attention. Try to sing this serenade and then listen to a recording of the piece. Note how Mozart uses a mandolin accompanied by *pizzicato* (plucked) strings to represent the accompanying instrument played on stage by Don Giovanni.

Don Giovanni courts Donna Anna

Canzonetta [simple solo song]
Allegretto [Quite lively, but not too fast]

Look down from out your win-dow, I now im-plore you, O fair-est of the fair, and hear my sigh-ing! Your fa-vour grant to me, who stand be-fore you, Or here your own dear eyes will see me dy-ing. Though hon-ey sweet lies hid-den deep in ro-ses, Sweet-er far is the hon-ey your mouth dis-clos-es! No lon-ger, la-dy fair, to me be cru-el, Throw me one glance, I pray, my love-ly jew-el!

FOLLOW UP

Mozart was one of the famous child prodigies in European musical history. Make a list of other well-known composers featured in *Portraits in Music* who showed great talent at an early age.

The study in Mozart's house in Salzburg

A London Newspaper Advertisement in 1765

The greatest Prodigy that Europe, or that even Human Nature has to boast of is, without Contradiction, the little German Boy, Wolfgang Mozart; a Boy, eight years old, who has, and indeed very justly, raised the Admiration not only of the greatest Men, but also of the greatest Musicians in Europe. It is hard to say whether his execution on the Harpsichord, and his playing and singing at Sight, or his own Caprice, Fancy and Compositions for all Instruments, are most astonishing. The Father of this Miracle, being obliged by Desire of several Ladies and Gentlemen, to postpone, for a very short time, his Departure from England, will give an Opportunity to hear this little Composer and his Sister, whose Musical knowledge wants not Apology. Performs every day in the Week, from Twelve to Three o'Clock in the Great Room, at the Swan and Hoop, Cornhill. Admittance 2/6 each Person.

'The two Children will play also together with four hands upon the same Harpsichord, and put upon it a Handkerchief, without seeing the Keys.'

(Public Advertiser, 11 July 1765)

The young Beethoven playing to Mozart

Wohin? ('Whither?')

SONG FROM 'DIE SCHÖNE MÜLLERIN'
('THE FAIR MAID OF THE MILL')

BY FRANZ SCHUBERT (1797-1828)

The following announcement was made in a leading Vienna newspaper in May 1808:

> NOTICE: As in the Royal Court Chapel there are two vacancies for singing boys, any one who wishes to occupy one of these positions should appear at three o'clock on the afternoon of 30 September, at the Royal Convict School, 796, University Square, prepared to undergo examination both as to progress in general education and also knowledge of music and bringing with him his school certificates.
>
> Competitors must have completed their tenth year and be capable of taking their place in the first Grammar Class.
>
> If the accepted boys distinguish themselves in conduct and studies, they will, according to royal ordinance, remain in the Convict School after their change of voice; otherwise after change of voice, they will leave the school.

'Convict' in this sense means 'boarding'. Boys accepted for a place in the royal choir received a general education at the school known as the Royal Boarding School. One of the two successful competitors in 1808 was an 11-year-old boy soprano called Franz Peter Schubert. Schubert was the son of a schoolmaster. The Schubert family was a very musical one and, every week, friends and neighbours assembled at their home to make music. Young Franz was taught to play the violin by his father and played in the small orchestra at these musical evenings. From an early age he also composed music and his friends at the Royal Boarding School performed his pieces.

On leaving school, Schubert attended a Training School for Teachers for a year before joining the staff at his father's school. He later resigned to devote himself to composing music, especially songs. Though his compositions got into print, Schubert was badly underpaid by his publishers: for a song or piano piece he sometimes received no more than five pence and sometimes could not afford to buy music manuscript paper. His friends, aware of his difficulties, printed some of his new songs and sold copies to audiences at concerts attended by the composer's admirers.

Among Schubert's music are symphonies, piano pieces, choral music, chamber music—and over six hundred songs. Despite his many compositions, Schubert was a poor man when he died in 1828 in Vienna at the age of 31.

Schubert accompanying a friend singing at a musical evening

SCHUBERT'S SONGS

Many of Schubert's songs were discovered in manuscript after his death—many others, unfortunately, were lost. In 1815, when he was 18 years old, Schubert composed 146 songs—30 in August, and 20 in October. Fifteen of them were written within two days. His songs have beautiful and most expressive piano accompaniments and the kind of song he composed is known in German as the **'Lied'**. Schubert was the greatest composer of **'Lieder'**. Some of these songs are short, some long, some with the same music for each verse and others **'through-composed'**, that is, with different music for the verses to suit the different meanings of the words. Many of his songs are 'lyrical' with lovely and expressive melodies, while others are highly dramatic with descriptive accompaniments. Some of the songs are arranged in 'cycles' (sets) and one of his most famous cycles is *The Fair Maid of the Mill*, made up of 26 songs and composed in the years 1823 and 1824.

DIE SCHÖNE MÜLLERIN
(The Fair Maid of the Mill)

Wilhelm Müller was the author of the poems that form Schubert's song cycle. The poems tell the tragic story of a young miller's love for his master's daughter. His thoughts and feelings about the girl he sings in moments of solitude to the mill-stream which becomes a sort of 'companion' to the youth and takes on an important role in the drama. At first all goes well but then the girl meets and falls in love with another admirer. The young miller returns to the brook, confides his sorrow to it, and finally, heartbroken, drowns himself in the brook's cool waters.

An ornate cover from an edition of Schubert's 'The Fair Maid of the Mill' printed in 1877

GUIDE TO THE MUSIC

Wohin? (Whither?) is the second song of the cycle. The young miller has left his home to wander freely like the restless mill-stream. He walks by the brook as it tumbles down the hillside and asks the brook to guide him on his way.

The song structure is 'through-composed'. The vocal phrases throughout most of the song are all four bars long and in the piano accompaniment the restless, flowing brook is portrayed in fast-moving, continuous semiquavers. The following is a bar-by-bar analysis of the song. Learn to sing the song and notice how Schubert develops the music.

FIRST SECTION

Bars 1- 2   Piano introduction—the rushing water of the brook.
Bars 3- 6   First appearance of a recurring vocal phrase.
Bars 7-10   Repetition of the vocal phrase.
Bars 11-14   Change of key.
Bars 15-18   Altered version of recurring vocal phrase.
Bars 19-22   Repetition of bars 15-18.

SECOND SECTION

Bars 23-26   Change of key.
Bars 27-30   New phrase—the rushing waters gather strength.
Bars 31-34   Modified version of bars 27-30.
Bars 35-39   Change of key.
Bars 40-41   The young miller repeats his urgent question.

Bars 42-45 Altered version of bars 23-26.
Bars 46-49 Repetition of bars 27-30 but this time in the minor key.
Bars 50-53 Lead into . . .

THIRD SECTION

Bars 54-57 Slightly altered version of bars 3-6.
Bars 58-61 Slightly altered version of bars 7-10.
Bars 62-65 As bars 23-26.
Bars 66-69 Altered version of bars 31-34.
Bars 70-73 Modified version of bars 66-69.
Bars 74-81 An extended version of bars 15-18—the miller follows the brook towards the mill and his fateful meeting with the girl.

FOLLOW UP

Listen to the following songs from *The Fair Maid of the Mill* and in your own words describe how Schubert illustrates the dramatic ideas of the story of the song cycle in his music.

Song 1:   *Wandering.* The young miller leaves his home to wander freely like the mill stream that never rests.

Song 5:   *Evening Rest.* At the end of the day's work the mill-owner and his daughter bid all the workmen goodnight, and the young miller wishes that he had a thousand arms to do the work so that he might impress her more than the others.

Song 7:   *Impatience.* The young miller is impatient to tell the whole world of his love for the miller's daughter.

Song 14: *The Huntsman.* The young miller's rival for the affections of the miller's daughter appears on the scene.

Song 19: *The Miller and the Brook.* The stream tries to console the broken-hearted lover.

WEST SIDE STORY

MUSICAL

BY LEONARD BERNSTEIN (b. 1918)

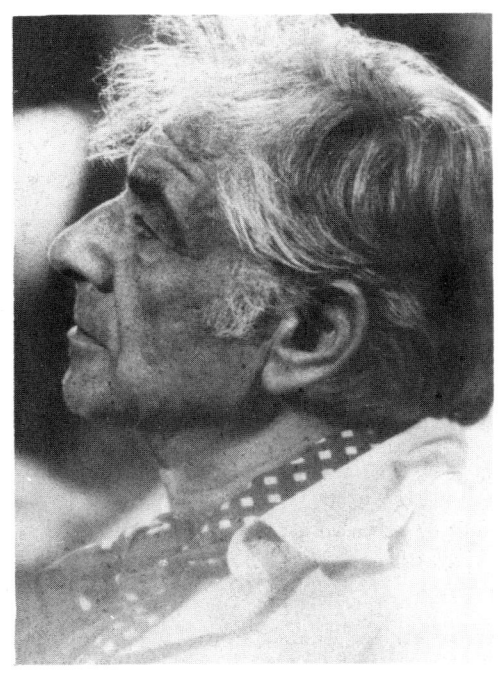

Leonard Bernstein was born in Lawrence, Massachusetts, on 25 August 1918. His parents were Russian immigrants. He graduated from Harvard College in 1939, shortly before his 21st birthday, enrolled as a student at the Curtis Institute in Philadelphia and studied with Serge Koussevitzky, the famous conductor of the Boston Symphony Orchestra. In 1943 he was appointed assistant conductor of the New York Philharmonic Orchestra.

Later that year, deputising for guest conductor Bruno Walter, who was suddenly taken ill, Bernstein, aged 25, experienced a sensational overnight success at a concert broadcast throughout the United States. All of a sudden he was the most sought-after young conductor in America. From 1945 to 1948 he was conductor of the New York City Symphony Orchestra and, in 1948, for a short time conducted the Israel Philharmonic Orchestra, often for Israeli troops at the front line in the first war with the Arabs. In 1958 at the age of 40, he became the first-ever American to direct a leading United States orchestra when he was made conductor of the New York Philharmonic Orchestra. Bernstein is a man of great energy: he is well-known as a conductor, composer, lecturer, and broadcaster. His compositions include ballet scores, symphonies, and works for the American musical stage.

West Side Story is Bernstein's most popular musical. It is a modern version of the story of Romeo and Juliet, transferred from its setting in medieval Verona to the slums of west-side New York of the 1960s. The ancient family feud between the Montagues and the Capulets becomes a struggle between two rival teenage gangs, the Jets and the Sharks. Romeo and Juliet are replaced by the young lovers, Tony and Maria. The famous balcony scene in Shakespeare's play is relocated on the fire-escape of a squalid New York tenement. The drama is played out in the violent backstreets of New York and dance is an important element in the action. The **choreography** (sequence of dance movements) for the Broadway show was by Jerome Robbins who made use of ballet and modern dance techniques in his often aggressive and at times quite terrifying routines involving the rival gangs.

The Sharks (see next page) dance through the streets of New York. George Chakiris (centre) plays their leader Bernardo

THE STORY

The curtain opens on a warehouse scene. During the opening minutes of the action not a word is spoken. Instead, members of the rival gangs are involved in a long dance sequence. This helps establish the sinister mood not only of the scene itself but also for the drama to come. One of the gangs, the Jets, guards its territory against invasion by its rivals, the Sharks, a gang made up entirely of Puerto Ricans. The gangs arrange a meeting at a dance held in the local gymnasium: at this meeting they will organise a time, place and weapons for a gang fight or 'rumble'. At the dance, Maria, the sister of Bernardo, leader of the Sharks, meets Tony, a member of the Jets. They fall in love; but belonging to enemy gangs they are forced to meet in great secrecy. They escape from the grim reality of their lives into a fanciful dream world. As he walks home alone from the dance, Tony sings about his love for Maria.

Tony stands outside the rooms where Maria lives with her parents and quietly whistles to attract her attention. She comes on to the fire escape. In 'Tonight' they sing of their meeting at the dance, Maria standing on the steps, with Tony, in the street, looking up at her.

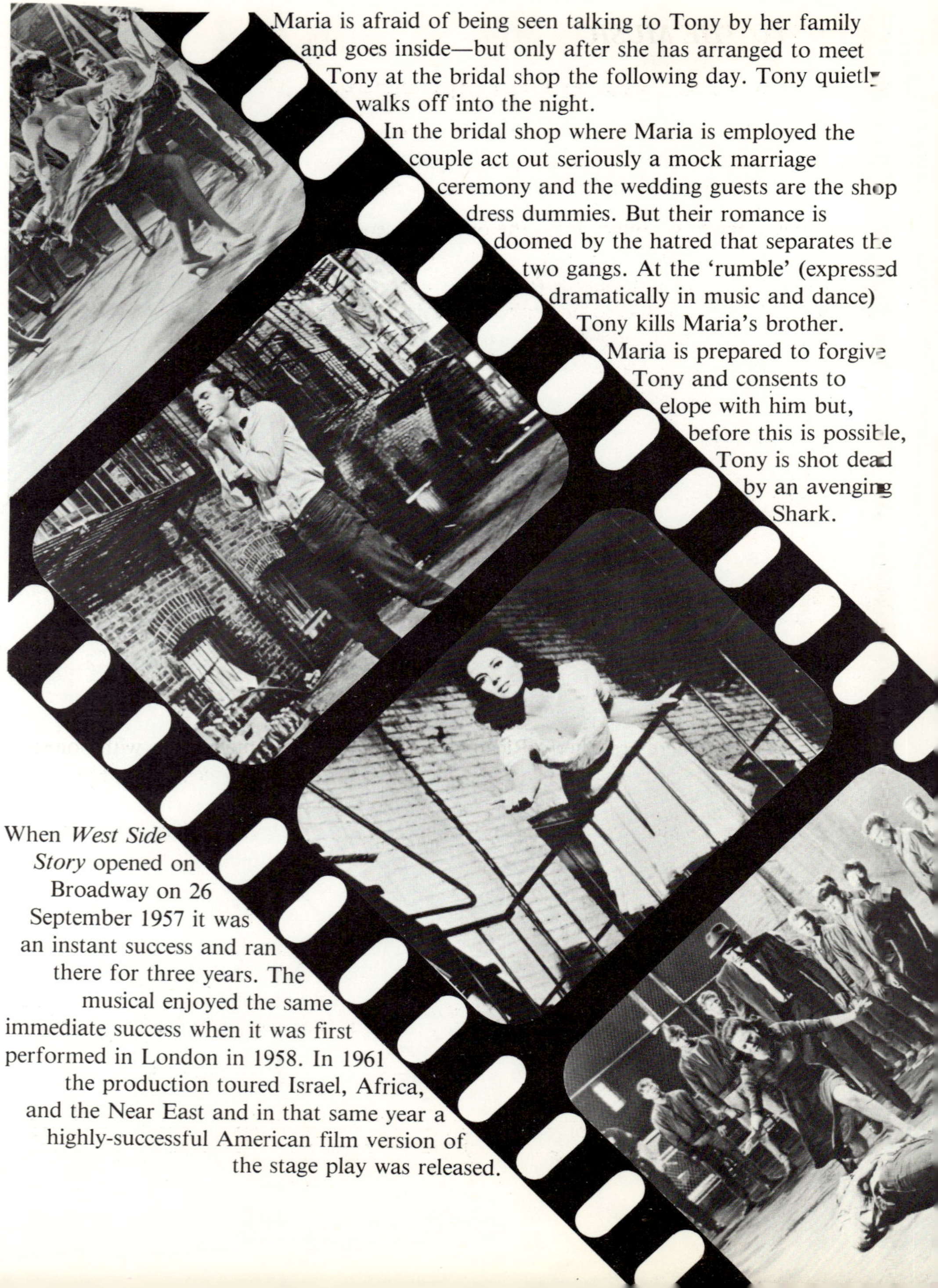

Maria is afraid of being seen talking to Tony by her family and goes inside—but only after she has arranged to meet Tony at the bridal shop the following day. Tony quietly walks off into the night.

In the bridal shop where Maria is employed the couple act out seriously a mock marriage ceremony and the wedding guests are the shop dress dummies. But their romance is doomed by the hatred that separates the two gangs. At the 'rumble' (expressed dramatically in music and dance) Tony kills Maria's brother.

Maria is prepared to forgive Tony and consents to elope with him but, before this is possible, Tony is shot dead by an avenging Shark.

When *West Side Story* opened on Broadway on 26 September 1957 it was an instant success and ran there for three years. The musical enjoyed the same immediate success when it was first performed in London in 1958. In 1961 the production toured Israel, Africa, and the Near East and in that same year a highly-successful American film version of the stage play was released.

GUIDE TO THE MUSIC

SYMPHONIC DANCES FROM WEST SIDE STORY

Listen to the *Symphonic Dances* which Leonard Bernstein wrote for orchestra based on music for *West Side Story*. To guide you in your listening, the following plan shows how the music of the *Symphonic Dances* is related to songs and incidents from the musical.

1. Prologue. Based on music from the opening scene of the musical, much of the music is made up of detached chords, bits of tune (played by a saxophone) and finger-snaps. The pace of the music quickens as the rival gangs taunt each other to the point where fighting breaks out and has to be broken up by the police. (*Listen for the police whistle*).
2. 'Somewhere'. The melody of this song is introduced by string and harp, producing a quiet, reflective atmosphere.

The music builds up to a climax before it gradually speeds up into . . .

3. Dance music. There are Puerto Rican elements in the instrumentation, with bongo drums particularly prominent in the percussion section. The music becomes brutal, energetic, loud.
4. 'Maria'. The quieter mood resumes with a light, delicate scoring of this song from the musical. (*Listen for the Indian bell*.)
5. 'Cool'.

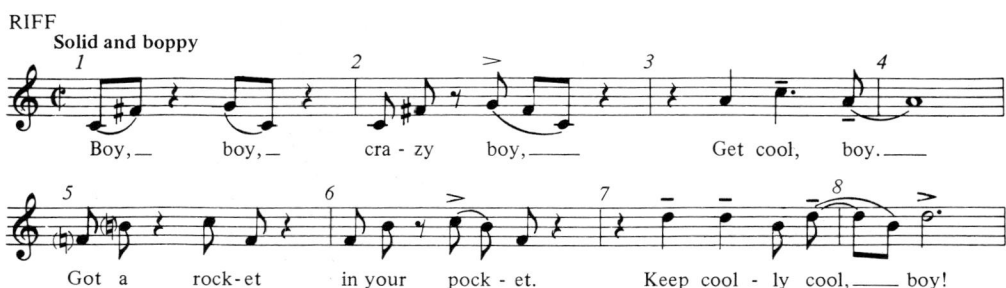

The music begins quietly but soon there are sudden outbursts and with menacing references to 'Somewhere' the music becomes restless and full of aggression.
6. There is a return to the music of the Prologue.
7. By contrast there follows a quiet, reflective episode built on fragments of the tune 'Somewhere'. After a climax the *Symphonic Dances* end peacefully.

The saxophone

Saxophones come in different sizes, but the most popular member of the family is the alto saxophone, shown here.

The saxophone was invented by the Belgian instrument-maker, Adolphe Sax, in 1840. It was first used in French military bands but gained its enormous popularity with the rise of Jazz from the 1890s on.

The saxophone belongs to the woodwind family despite the fact that it is made of metal. Its bore is conical like the oboe, and it has a single reed like the clarinet. Being a hybrid instrument its tone is very flexible and expressive; this characteristic makes the saxophone a very useful instrument in military bands since it blends well with either woodwind or brass instruments.

In jazz, the saxophone frequently has 'slinky' tunes to play and Bernstein exploits this side of its character in the Prologue music of his *Symphonic Dances*.

The Romeo and Juliet story has formed the basis of works by a number of different composers: besides Bernstein, Tchaikovsky was attracted to the story's opposing ideas of love between individuals and conflict between groups. Listen to Tchaikovsky's *Romeo and Juliet*. Which composer do you think portrays (a) love and (b) violence more effectively?

Prelude to
The Mastersingers of Nuremberg

BY RICHARD WAGNER (1813-1883)

Richard Wagner was born in Leipzig, East Germany, in 1813. When he was only six months old, his father died and his mother remarried. Wagner's stepfather, a very kind man, was an actor and playwright and, through his influence, the teenage Wagner became very interested in literature and drama. He studied musical composition at Leipzig and through his interests in music and drama was attracted to opera. At the age of 20, he was appointed choir trainer at the opera house in Würzburg. A year later he became conductor of the opera house in Magdeburg and thereafter at the opera houses of Königsberg and Riga.

In 1842 his first major opera *Rienzi* was performed in Dresden. As with all his succeeding works, Wagner not only wrote the music but also the words. *Rienzi* was an immediate success and was followed by *The Flying Dutchman, Tannhäuser,* and *Lohengrin.*

During 1848-49 there were revolutions throughout Europe. Wagner took part in an unsuccessful rebellion at Dresden and to avoid arrest had to make a swift escape from the city. He settled in Switzerland for some years and in 1860 was told that he could safely return to Germany. He was invited by young King Ludwig II of Bavaria to stay in Munich but the jealousies of courtiers drove him to leave and return to Switzerland. In 1872, aged 59, Wagner settled in the little Bavarian town of Bayreuth and financial support from admirers in different countries helped him to build there a theatre specially designed for the performance of his own works. The theatre was opened in 1876 and his great operas, *The Mastersingers of Nuremberg, Tristan and Isolde, Parsifal,* and *The Ring of the Nibelung* (a series of four works), all composed during his periods in Switzerland, were performed there. In 1883, suffering from ill health, he spent the winter in Venice where he died suddenly at the age of 69.

He was buried in the garden of his villa in Bayreuth. Performances of his operas continue to be presented in his theatre, now directed by members of his family, at an annual Bayreuth festival.

Wagner's opera *The Mastersingers* is set in 16th-century Nuremberg, the capital of Bavaria. The city's ancient guild of Mastersingers is led by a good-natured and talented shoemaker, Hans Sachs, who also is a poet, playwright, and composer. The guild's members are tradesmen and craftsmen who love and practise music and who are bound to observe the rules of the guild. (These guilds were found in many German cities and towns in the 14th, 15th, and 16th centuries. Wagner's work is based on real people—Hans Sachs was a famous shoemaker/Mastersinger of Nuremburg. He lived there from 1494 to 1576 and is said to have written 4,000 songs!). The story centres round a Song Contest attended by the entire population of Nuremberg. The prize for the winning song is the hand in marriage of the lovely Eva, daughter of a goldsmith. There are two contestants: the first is the foolish town clerk, Beckmesser, who writes songs in a traditional style, paying attention to an elaborate set of rules; the second is a young knight, Walther von Stolzing, who has new and exciting ideas about song-writing. Walther, with the encouragement of Hans Sachs, wins the contest and his beautiful prize.

The Bayreuth Festival Theatre, founded in 1876 by Richard Wagner for the performance of his operas

GUIDE TO THE MUSIC

The *Prelude* sets the mood for the rest of the opera. The piece begins with the majestic theme of the guild of the Mastersingers (**A**):

The Mastersingers theme is extended by the full orchestra to a climax and after this it makes way for a theme associated in the opera with Walther's love for Eva:

Then follows a second theme (**B**) representing the guild, a march-like tune which Wagner adapted from a traditional Mastersingers melody that he discovered in an ancient book dealing with their customs.

Now comes a passage based on the Mastersingers first theme (**A**) which combines many orchestral strands in a rich web of sound:

This is followed by a theme associated with Walther which in Act 3 of the opera becomes part of his Prize Song.

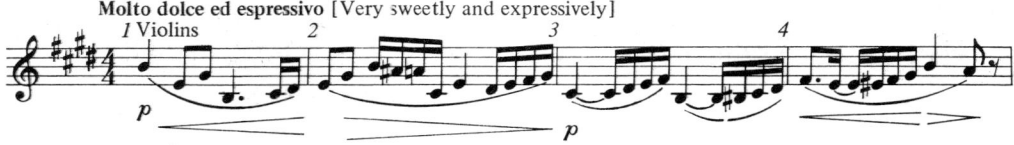

This theme is interrupted by one associated with Walther's impatience.

The mood suddenly changes and Wagner introduces a playful version of the Mastersingers theme—this is the theme associated in the opera with the Apprentices who are making fun of the older and more dignified fully-fledged members of the guild. Note how the tunes of the Mastersingers and their Apprentices are closely related:

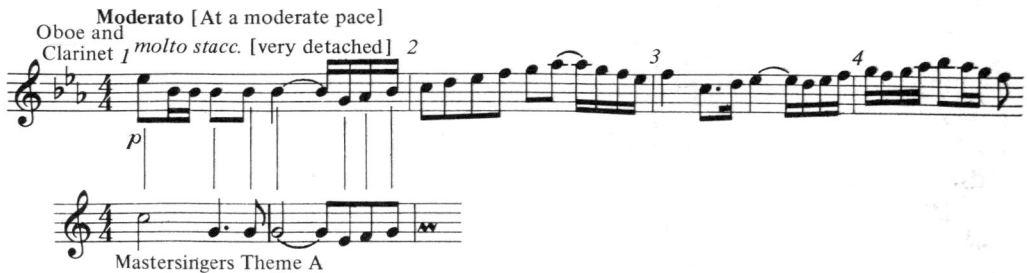

Now comes the return of the Mastersingers theme (**A**) and the end of the Prelude. At this point, Wagner combines in his music melodies representing three different characters or ideas—can you identify them played separately by your teacher, then together played by the orchestra?

The Prelude finishes with the Mastersingers theme (**A**) followed by triumphant fanfares.

Musical characterisation

From looking at the Prelude you will have noticed that Wagner uses short musical themes (**leitmotifs** in German) to represent characters and ideas from his story. These are welded together in the opera to form a musical accompaniment to the action on stage. For example, when the Mastersingers appear or are referred to in the opera their *motif* forms the basis of the musical accompaniment. Such means of composing helped Wagner to free himself from the strict divisions into **song, chorus** and **recitative** which had restricted operatic composers up till this time. (See Verdi's *Rigoletto* in *Portraits in Music I* page 8.)

FOLLOW UP

For Wagner, Walther's *Prize Song* was obviously an important climax in his operatic design for *The Mastersingers*. In Act 1, Scene 3, Wagner gives a clear picture of how to compose a Mastersong. The rules of the 16th-century Mastersingers' guild are, in fact, quoted by Köthner (a member of the guild):

Woodcut of Hans Sachs, the famous shoemaker, poet and Mastersinger of Nuremberg

> 'Each unit of a Mastersong shall present a proper balance of its different sections, . . . against which no one shall offend. A section consists of two stanzas which shall have the same melody; the stanza is a group of so many lines, the line has its rhyme at the end. Thereupon follows the Aftersong which is also to be so many lines long and have its own special melody which is not to occur in the stanza. Each Mastersong shall have several units in this ratio; and whoever composes a new song which does not for more than four syllables encroach upon other Masters' melodies, his song may win a Master's prize.'

Learn to sing Walther's *Prize Song* and decide if Walther, in planning his Mastersong, has cast his poem in the form required by the guild.

The composer Franz Liszt playing to Wagner and a group of friends

Walther's Prize Song from Act 3 Scene 5 — Original Key: C

Moderato molto [At a very moderate pace]

Morn-ing was glow-ing in splen-dour of light, The fra-grant breeze per-fumed the leas, Where, bright with flow-ers, twined in bow-ers, A gar-den charmed my sight; And there be-neath a won-drous tree, With gold-en fruit o'er-la-den, My dream-land fan-cies showed to me A beaut-eous ten-der maid-en, The love-light in her eyes; My heart's de-sire, Eva, in Pa-ra-dise.

SYMPHONY NO. 9 IN E MINOR (FROM THE NEW WORLD)

BY ANTONÍN DVOŘÁK (1841-1904)

Antonín Dvořák was born in a village near Prague in 1841. His father was a butcher and a publican, and Dvořák, when he was a boy, helped his father in the butcher's shop. At that time his interest in music began as he listened to his father playing the zither and to travelling bands as they passed through the village. Dvořák learned to play the violin and later had piano and organ lessons. At the age of 16 he went to Prague and studied organ at a school run by the Bohemian Church Music Society. To earn a living, he played the viola in city cafes and was organist at a lunatic asylum; he was very poor and could not even afford to buy music or attend concerts. In 1862, Dvořák became a member of the viola section of the orchestra of the newly-established National Theatre of Prague, but continued to compose in his spare time. About ten years later he left the orchestra to take up a good appointment as church organist and, around the same time, he married. His music was now attracting attention in Europe, and he received much support and encouragement from the composer Brahms. From 1892-95 he was appointed head of the National Conservatory in New York. He then returned to Prague where, a few years later, he was appointed head of the Conservatory. His music includes symphonies, operas, concertos, chamber music, and choral pieces. He died in Prague in 1904, aged 62.

DVOŘÁK IN THE 'NEW WORLD'

In the summer of 1891, Dvořák was offered the post of Director of the National Conservatory of Music of America, in New York. Because of his many European commitments and his attachment to his native country, Dvořák spent several months carefully considering the offer. By Christmas, however, he had made up his mind to accept and, in September 1892, with his wife and two elder children, he left for New York.

By 1892, the National Conservatory of Music of America had been in existence for seven years. The President of the Conservatory, Mrs Jeanette Thurber, an energetic and strong-willed lady, wanted to establish a music institution in America which would rival the great conservatories of Paris and Leipzig, she decided that it required a Director who was internationally famous, and that Dvořák was the person for the job. Dvořák, when first approached, was not too enthusiastic about the appointment and declined it. But Mrs Thurber, not easily put off, renewed the offer and made it so attractive in financial terms that the composer could not refuse.

In America, Dvořák conducted public concerts in New York and other cities and, though involved in teaching and examining at the Conservatory, was given much free time to spend as he wished. During the Columbus Fourth Centennial celebrations he conducted a performance of his *Te Deum* which he had composed before leaving for America. At first, the homesick Dvořák found it difficult to settle down in his new surroundings. Mrs Thurber, to help keep up his spirits, took him to see the Red Indian dances in Buffalo Bill's Wild West Show in the hope that he might write a Hiawatha opera. However, by the end of the year, Dvořák had started to work on new compositions and in May 1893 he completed the first of his American pieces—his symphony 'From the New World'.

Dvořák's house in New York

Travels in America

Throughout his stay in America, Dvořák suffered from homesickness—he missed his friends, his country and, most of all, his four youngest children. When he heard that his children had reached Southampton on their way to join him in America for the summer vacation, he was so excited that he forgot to complete the trombone parts in the final bars of the 'New World' Symphony and did not find out about his omission until the piece was being rehearsed some months later! During that long summer vacation Dvořák was happiest when staying in the Czech settlement at Spillville, Iowa. During his visit to Spillville he met some Indians and invited them to meet his family whom they entertained with songs and dances. He also attended Czech Day at the World Fair, in Chicago, where 30,000 Czechs from all parts of the United States took part in a grand parade.

Dvořák's contract expired in 1894 but the persuasive Mrs. Thurber managed to get him to agree to renew his contract for a further two years. However, in 1895, suffering increasingly from homesickness and missing his family, Dvořák finally decided that it was impossible for him to return for the winter of 1895-96.

The 'New World' Symphony

The first performance of the 'New World' Symphony, conducted by Anton Seidl on 16 December 1893 at New York's famous Carnegie Hall was an immediate success. Dvořák was elated and wrote to his publisher, Simrock, in Prague, telling him about the marvellous newspaper reports on the piece and its composer, and the tumultuous applause from the audience which made him fell like a king sitting in his box.

Dvořák and his family on the steps of their home in New York

NEW YORK HERALD

26 December 1893

Dr. Dvořák's Great Symphony

The Director of the National Conservatory adds a masterpiece to musical literature

Inspired by Indian music

Small wonder that the listeners were enthusiastic. The work appealed to their sense of the pathetically beautiful by its wealth of tender, pathetic, fiery melody; by its rich harmonic clothing; by its delicate, sonorous, gorgeous, every varying instrumentation.

It has been suggested that Dvořák used original American national and Indian melodies in his symphony. This is untrue—Dvořák himself called the suggestion a load of nonsense. But it is clear that America, a young and vigorous nation with vast frontiers, impressed Dvořák and inspired him to write a symphony which has a tremendous feeling of the outdoors. Dvořák himself wrote that if he had not seen America he would never have written the symphony in the way he did. And a report in the *New York Herald* on the symphony's first performance describes the work as 'a distinctive American work in so far as it gave the Czech composer's impression of the country'. It would seem that his native land was never far from Dvořák's mind.

The first sketches of the 'New World' Symphony were begun in December 1892 and, a month later, Dvořák had sketched out the first three movements which he orchestrated in the early months of 1893. In May of that year he wrote and orchestrated the last movement. The pleasure he experienced in writing the symphony sounds out from every page of the score.

GUIDE TO THE MUSIC

The symphony begins with a slow, sombre introduction. The mood suddenly changes and leads to the faster main section of the movement which has three melodies.

The development (middle section) is based on tunes **(C)** and **(A)**. From the following extract you can separate elements of the two melodies:

In the recapitulation (final section) the three tunes are played again and the movement comes to a vigorous conclusion.

SECOND MOVEMENT

According to the composer this movement was inspired by Minnehaha's funeral in the forest in Longfellow's poem *The Song of Hiawatha*.

The slow movement begins with a solemn progression of chords played by brass instruments, clarinets and bassoons,

which introduces a lovely melody played by the cor anglais:

In the middle section two new melodies are heard.

These melodies are repeated and are followed by woodwind imitation of bird-songs. In a moment of drama, the trombones remind us of the opening tune of the first movement.

The final section of the movement brings a shortened version of the cor anglais melody and the solemn brass chords, heard at the start of the movement, reppear in the closing bars.

THIRD MOVEMENT

Dvořák said that this movement was suggested by the scene at the feast in Longfellow's poem where the Indians dance and, in the music, he tried to impart some Indian 'colour'.

This scherzo begins with a lively tune presented in canon (like a round):

A new, slower melody is introduced by flute and oboe:

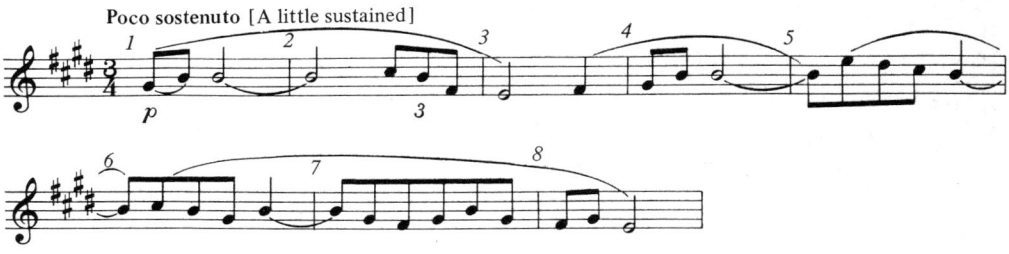

The middle section of the movement is built on a tune which has a (Bohemian?) country dance character:

The opening section is repeated and is followed by a **coda** (concluding passage) which features tunes (**A**) and (**C**) of the *first* movement in combination with the opening tune of the scherzo.

FOURTH MOVEMENT

A build-up of nine stormy bars leads into the finale's first theme, a solemn melody played by trumpets and horns:

The violins then play a lively theme:

and the clarinet follows with a contrasting melody.

The **development** section begins quietly and fragments of the opening two melodies of the finale are joined by fragments of the opening melodies of preceding movements like threads in a tapestry coming together to form a new picture.

In a shortened **recapitulation** the second tune of the finale is left out, and in the coda there is further reference to melodies from all movements of the symphony. The piece comes to a heroic and exciting conclusion.

(You may need to remind yourself of how a symphony is built up. See *Portraits in Music I*, page 20.)

Dvořák, during his first months in New York, showed an interest in Negro songs and the cor anglais melody of the slow movement of his 'New World' Symphony seems to express something of their spirit. On the other hand, the composer was not an American, he was Czech; and the thoughts and feelings expressed in the symphony are those of a Czech and his music may be regarded as essentially Czech in character. Learn the famous Negro Spiritual, *Steal away,* and compare its rhythms, melody and structure with Dvořák's cor anglais melody. Do **you** think Dvořák intended to copy it in the 'New World' Symphony?

Steal away

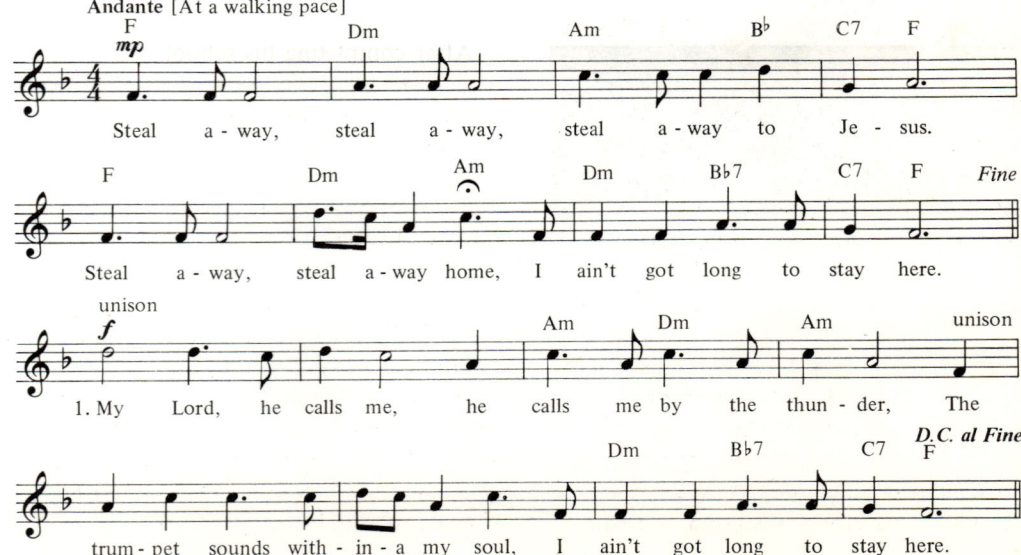

Polonaise in A flat major

PIANO PIECE

BY FRÉDÉRIC CHOPIN (1810-1849)

Frédéric Chopin was born in 1810 in a village near Warsaw; his mother was Polish and his father French. His father had left France at the age of 16 and worked as a French tutor in various noble Polish households before marrying.

Chopin was a child prodigy, and his first published composition appeared when he was seven. Despite the temptation to exploit his great musical talents his parents made sure that he had a good education and a sound musical training. There was little his teacher could show Chopin about the technical aspects of playing the piano but he instead developed the boy's inventiveness. He introduced Chopin to the music of Bach, Mozart and Beethoven.

Chopin's three earliest surviving works are Polonaises, suggesting that his love of traditional Polish music was present from the start. He began at the same time to play in the elegant aristocratic *salons* of Warsaw, surroundings which he found much more to his liking than vast concert halls to put across his particular style of music making.

After completing his school examinations in 1826 he undertook three years full-time study at the Warsaw Conservatory. Thereafter, he left Warsaw for ever and travelled by way of Munich and Vienna to Paris where he lived on money he made by teaching and performing and from sales of his compositions.

In 1836 he began a love affair with the authoress George Sand and for 11 years composed feverishly for the piano. In 1848 he made a concert tour of England and Scotland, but he was by this time a sick man. He died in Paris in October 1849 of tuberculosis.

Chopin's mistress, the authoress George Sand

CHOPIN AND THE PIANO

Chopin's reputation as a composer is based entirely on music involving the piano either as a solo or as an accompanying instrument. He composed some of the finest music of its type in every form in which he wrote.

- *Piano solo*
  10 Polonaises
  54 Mazurkas
  14 Waltzes
  19 Nocturnes
  25 Preludes
  27 Studies
  4 Ballades
  4 Scherzos
  3 Sonatas
  4 Impromptus

- *Piano and orchestra*
  2 piano concertos

  Variations on *Là ci darem...*
  (from Mozart's *Don Giovanni*)

- *Chamber music*
  Sonata } cello and
  Introduction and Polonaise } piano
  Duo
  Trio for piano, violin and cello

- *Vocal music*
  17 Polish songs

During the later 18th century public concerts had become more popular. The solo recital—especially for piano—was one of the most popular forms of concert during the Romantic period. (You can read more about Romantic music on page 11.) Chopin felt his talents wasted on concert audiences and preferred the appreciation of a cultured minority. This he found in the *salon*, that select gathering of fashionable and intellectual people which became so much a feature of the Parisian scene.

Perhaps the main point to stress when looking at Chopin's output is its sheer variety; in terms of mood, scope, range of dynamics, keyboard texture and tempo variations, Chopin's music is unique in exploring the range of possibilities of a single instrument.

GUIDE TO THE MUSIC

A dramatic, tension-building introduction, 16 bars long, leads to the first main tune of the Polonaise.

This is repeated more forcefully, scored widely for the piano.

Then comes an episode which, with dotted rhythms and military-like fanfares, sounds somewhat menacing. A nostalgic few bars of melody are accompanied by the typical rhythm of the Polonaise.

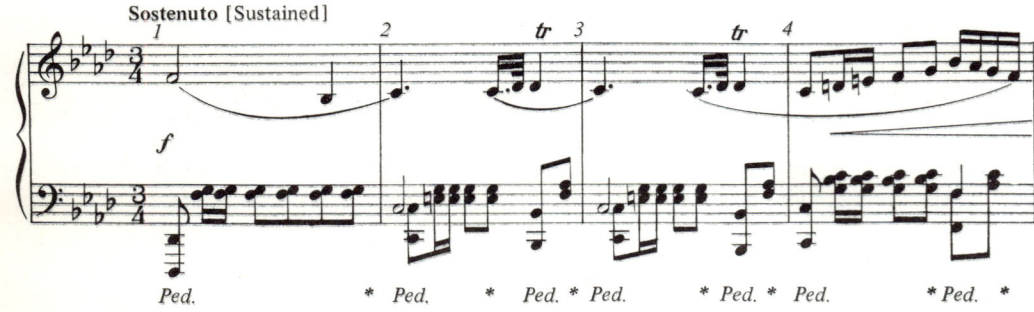

This leads without a break into a repetition of the main tune of the Polonaise, scored as on its second appearance.

Suddenly the music plunges from the key of A flat major into E major. The volume of the music drops to *pp* and over a repeated 4-note bass pattern a hushed melody is presented.

The very fast repetitions of the ostinato in the L.H., apparently simple and unobtrusive, are in fact extremely difficult for the pianist to play, firstly, because they go on so long (!) and secondly, because they must not overshadow the R.H. melody.

The music gradually increases in volume, slips down a semitone into E flat major and reaches a climax. E flat becomes D sharp and leads the music back to E major and the whole process begins again. The tonal 'side-step' into E flat occurs at the same point as before and a climax is reached.

A more soulful, nostalgic melody

leads on to a dreaming episode—the quiet before the storm?

Gradually tension mounts, culminating in the return of the opening theme, fully scored. A brilliant coda (tail piece) rounds off the Polonaise with a flourish. The 'tonal ambiguity' (A flat = G sharp and E flat = D sharp) which characterises this Polonaise is maintained even to the last few bars—a C major chord is set against the emphatic final chord in A flat major.

FOLLOW UP

Chopin playing the piano at the salon of Prince Antoine Radziwill in 1829

Listen to Chopin's *Polonaise in A major op. 40 No. 1* and try to follow the progress of the music as you listen on the following diagram of its musical organisation.

SECTION A

Theme A ⟶ Contrasting section (Theme B) ⟶ Theme A

⟶ **SECTION B**

Theme C ⟶ Contrasting section ⟶ Theme C

⟶ **SECTION A**

Theme A ⟶ Contrasting section (Theme B) ⟶ Theme A

The development of the piano

In Florence, at the beginning of the 18th century, Bartolomeo Cristofori, an Italian instrument-maker, combined the strings and hammers of the dulcimer with the keyboard of the harpsichord to produce the first *gravicembalo col piano e forte* (a 'harpsichord with quiet and loud')—in other words, he had invented the piano. As the original title implies it was possible to produce a variety of quiet and loud sounds, the volume of the sound depending on the force of the player's touch. The strings were struck by padded hammers which fell away from the strings leaving them free to vibrate.

The main areas in which instrument-makers have been seeking improvements since Cristofori's time include:

1. developing the keyboard and hammer mechanism to make it as responsive as possible to the player's touch, and

2. designing a suitable framework to withstand the enormous pressure of string tension.

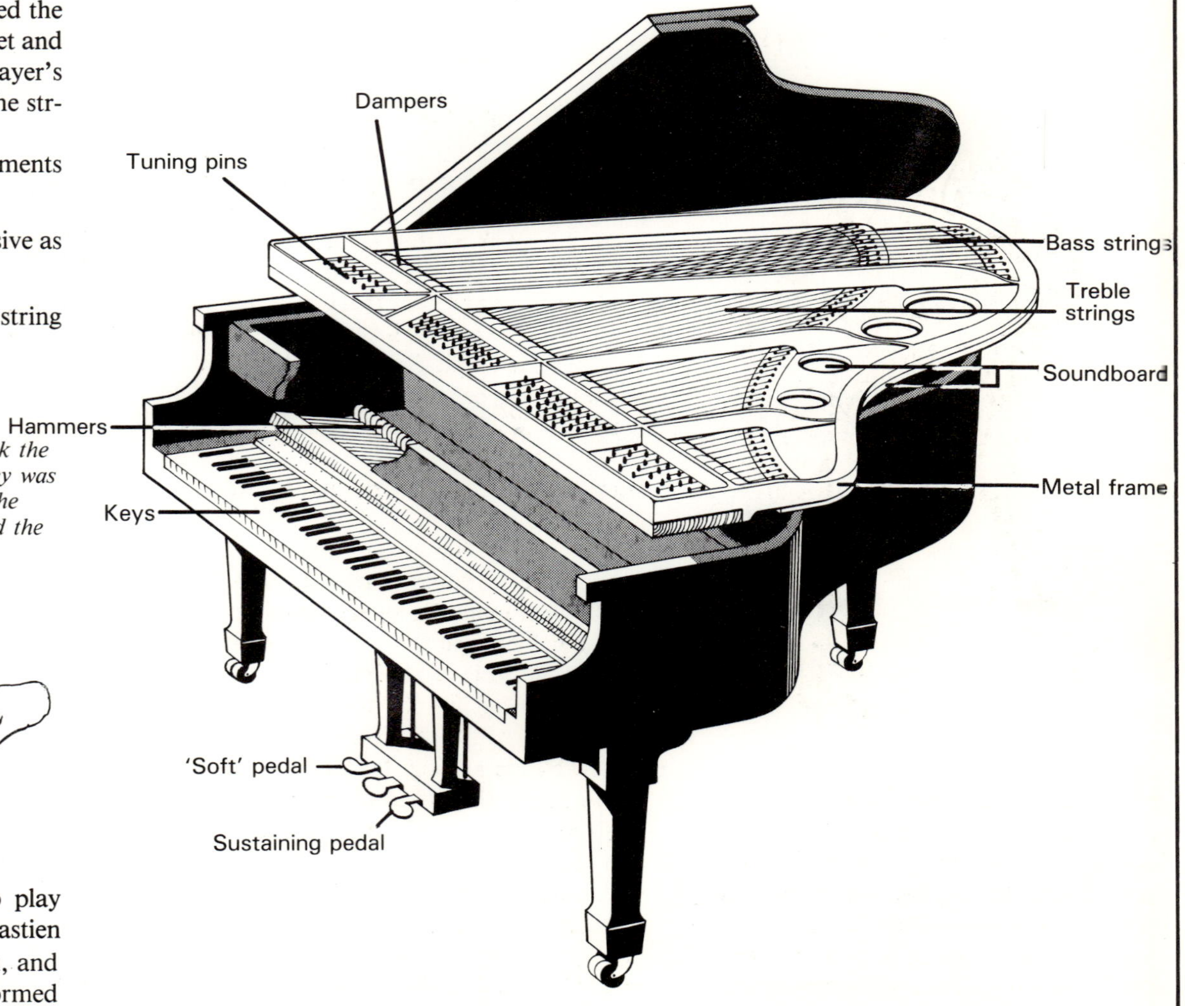

The escapement mechanism. When there was no escapement (a) the hammer struck the string when the key was pressed down and remained in contact with it until the key was released. With the invention of escapement (b) in the mid 1770s the hammer left the string directly and the string remained vibrating (sounding) until the player released the key.

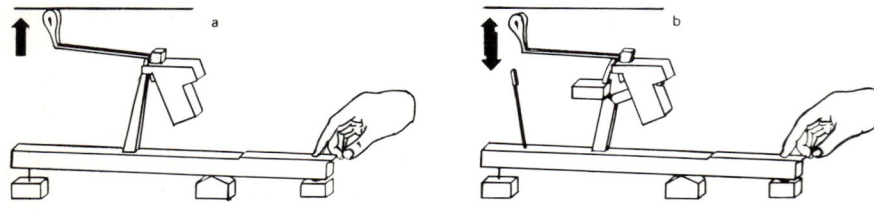

The invention of the **double escapement action** (enabling performers to play passages involving fast repeated notes without fully raising the key) by Sebastien Érard in Paris in 1821 ended the search for an effective striking mechanism, and the **metal frame** was patented in England in 1820. These two inventions formed the basis for the action of the modern piano and Chopin reaped the benefit of them in his piano music.

Tales from the Vienna Woods

WALTZ

BY JOHANN STRAUSS II (1825-1899)

Johann Strauss the elder lived from 1804 to 1849 and is largely responsible for the waltz's great popularity in Europe in the 19th century. During his lifetime he was unrivalled as a violinist and as a composer/conductor of light music. But after his death his reputation was eclipsed by that of his eldest son, Johann the younger. (His younger sons Joseph and Edward were also distinguished composers and conductors.)

The sons of Johann Strauss the elder did not find it easy to become musicians since their father strongly opposed their musical studies. He claimed he wanted to protect them from the financial insecurities of leading an artist's life. But the truth was probably that he feared they might become his rivals. That fear was, in fact, well founded, for when Johann the second made his café-house début at Donmayer's Casino in a suburb of Vienna on 15 October 1844, he created a sensation and immediately made a name for himself.

Politics soon increased the rift between Johann the second and his father. In 1848, when many European countries were rebelling against the rule of the Austrians, there was political unrest in Vienna, the capital of Austria. The young Johann sided with the Radicals, while his father, by composing the *Radetzky March* in honour of the Austrian general who had crushed the revolt in the Italian state of Lombardy, inevitably became linked with the reactionary party. These political associations were unjust because the Strausses were basically not politically-minded. In fact, Johann the elder met with such hostility when he appeared in public after 1848 that this may even have helped to hasten his death in the following year.

Johann the second continued his father's work, but soon found he was more suited to being a composer rather than a conductor—so he asked his brother Joseph to take over direction of the family orchestra.

Strauss playing at his first concert in 1844

DANCE IN THE 19th CENTURY

Standards of dancing in the early part of the 19th century were not as high as they might have been. Dancing was no longer considered a pastime or accomplishment that required constant practice and attention to details of performance.

The dances which were all the rage in the ballroom were the **waltz** and the **polka** (dances performed by two people), and reels, hornpipes, quadrilles, cotillons and country dances (dances performed by groups). Composers were not attracted by group dances because there was no opportunity to make money out of them. The sheet music publishers sold to the public very cheaply—24 new dances for a shilling, according to Thomas Wilson in his *Companion to the Ball Room* (London 1816). Royalties for the composer for one dance must have been negligible.

For this reason the waltz and the polka were the most popular dances with composers. Some dances from other countries found favour too, for example the **mazurka** and **polonaise** from Poland (Chopin), the **tarantella** and **saltarello** from Italy (Mendelssohn). The waltz probably derived from an Austrian dance called the *Ländler*. This was an old, slow, 3-time dance performed out of doors by dancers in heavy shoes. The steps of the waltz are characterised by sliding movements. To be performed effectively it required smooth ballroom floors and light shoes, and so had a generally more civilized appeal than the peasant *Ländler*.

The centre of dancing was waltz-mad Vienna and Johann Strauss the second was Vienna's 'waltz-king'. His music was the voice of its times. Austria at that time was ruled by the emperor Francis I, a dictator who employed a host of spies to inform him of any signs of uprising among the people. Austrians tended to avoid serious discussions—especially about politics—and they sought escapism in café-house gossip, light music, and dancing. This pleasure-seeking attitude to life which characterised the times under the Hapsburgs (the family name of the Austrian rulers) is echoed in Strauss's music.

GUIDE TO THE MUSIC

A lengthy introduction precedes the waltz selection. Horn calls suggest the pastoral atmosphere of the Vienna Woods; tentative quiet melodic fragments alternate with positive loud rhythmic phrases.

After a sustained chord, there is the first hint of a waltz melody to come—the second of the waltz sequence, in fact.

It is not long before an elaborate cadenza for flute pictures a feathered warbler of the Vienna Woods.

This leads to a repetition of the second waltz tune in Ländler tempo (slower than waltz tempo).

The pace of the music quickens in anticipation of the waltz, and, after an introductory *oom-pah-pah* to establish waltz tempo firmly, the first of the main waltz tunes is heard.

The second main waltz theme is familiar from the introduction—now played as a 'straight' waltz.

The third main waltz tune is in E flat major.

The fourth main waltz tune returns to B flat major and its central section is twittery.

The fifth waltz tune is in E flat major.

To round off the sequence there is a prolonged coda; a tension-building section is based on the rhythm of Waltz 4, but it is not long before the now-familiar strains of Waltz 1 are heard.

An off-beat episode—melodically of less significance—paves the way for Tune 2 of Waltz 2.

Another episode, based this time on the rhythm of Waltz 2

leads to an exciting version of the main tune of Waltz 2.

A final flurry, beginning quietly and rising rapidly to a climax, brings the Waltz sequence to a vigorous close in F major.

> Having seen it performed by a select party of foreigners, we could not help reflecting how uneasy an English mother would be to see her daughter so familiarly treated ...
> *Dr. Charles Burney*

> A Strauss waltz boasts more melodies than a symphony of Beethoven, and the sum of Strauss's melodies is surely greater than that of Beethoven's.
> *Paul Bekker*

A ball in progress in 1885

Other Strauss waltzes

The Blue Danube
A work inspired by Vienna's great river.

Acceleration
Waltz gets its name through the use of speeding up (*accelerando*) in the main waltz.

An Artist's Life
An impression of the 'ups and downs' of bohemian life.

Emperor Waltz
Written in 1888 to celebrate the 40th anniversary of the reign of Franz Joseph I. The main waltz suggests the grandeur of the Austrian Empire and the dignity of its monarch.

Morning Journals
It owes its inspiration to a set of waltzes by Jacques Offenbach called *Evening Journals*.

Roses from the South
A collection of tunes from Strauss's operetta *The Queen's Lace Handkerchief* composed in 1880.

Vienna Blood
In contrast to *Tales from the Vienna Woods* with its pastoral feeling, this waltz portrays the more emotional aspects of Viennese life.

Voices of Spring
A picture of spring; birds twitter in the trees and the sap rises at the birth of another year in nature.

Wine, Women and Song
This waltz has the longest introduction of any Strauss waltz (91 bars), a fact which has nothing to do with its title!

Cover of a famous collection of Strauss waltzes, 'Gartenlaube' (Summer house), printed in 1895

The waltz

The elements of waltz composition—strict tempo for dancing, monotonous oom-pah-pah accompaniment—force a composer to seek variety in his compositions by means of changing the keys in his music. Here is a plan which shows how Strauss achieves variety in his *Tales from the Vienna Woods*.

Introduction	Atmospheric opening (C major—A minor—G major) Waltz tune 2 (G major) Cadenza Repeat Pace quickens (D major—G major—C major)
Waltz 1	F major
Waltz 2	B flat major
Waltz 3	E flat major
Waltz 4	B flat major
Waltz 5	E flat major
Coda	Waltz tune 4 (B flat major) Waltz tune 1 (F major) Middle of Waltz tune 2 (B flat major) Waltz tune 2 (F major) Final flourish (F major)

You will notice how the set waltz sequence is less flexible than the music of the introduction and the coda. So it is in these sections that the composer can be at his most creative.

The pattern we have observed in *Tales from the Vienna Woods* is typical of Johann Strauss's waltz compositions, the structure of which can be summed up as follows:

1. An **introduction**, frequently quite extensive, which introduces some of the waltz themes (or fragments of them) before the main sequence of tunes begins.
2. **A succession of waltz melodies**, one blending naturally into the next. (Normally there were at least five waltzes in a sequence.)
3. A **coda**—a kind of summing-up—providing a 'last look' at some of the basic waltz tunes.

FOLLOW UP

Improvise a simple waltz tune over the following chord progression.

$\frac{3}{4}$

B flat	B flat	E flat	E flat
F	F	B flat	B flat
B flat	E flat	E flat	E flat
F	F	B flat	B flat	

Some suggestions for instrumentation

1. Use one instrument to play the bass line, e.g. cello.
2. Use one instrument to play the melody you compose, e.g. flute.
3. Use one instrument to play the harmony, e.g. guitar.
   If you are using guitar rewrite the chord sequence substituting A for B flat, D for E flat, and E for F, and place a capo at the first fret.
4. Use percussion instruments to reinforce the 'oom-pah-pah' rhythm of the accompaniment.

Once you have completed your waltz turn to p. 44 and compare your piece with what Johann Stauss wrote using similar harmonies.

THE BARTERED BRIDE

OPERA

BY BEDŘICH SMETANA (1824-1884)

Bedřich Smetana was born in Bohemia (now Czechoslovakia) in 1824. He was the son of a village brewer. Though he was almost 40 years old before he completed his first opera, he had become well known as a talented musician at a much earlier age. As a child he performed piano pieces composed for such virtuoso instrumentalists as Liszt. Aged four he took part in a string quartet! He had only one ambition—to be a musician.

From the time when the 19-year-old Smetana moved to Prague he became familiar with the music of the great Viennese masters, Mozart and Beethoven. To this was added an enthusiasm for Schumann, Chopin and especially Liszt whom he had heard playing in 1840. Berlioz (see p. 8) visited Prague in 1846 and Smetana met him on that occasion. Side by side with these important foreign influences went the emergence of a national artistic conscience in Czechoslovakia. Smetana was sensitive to and sympathetic with both aspects. The works which he wrote in the revolutionary year of 1848 particularly show these influences and bear similarities with the literary works of many writers and artists of the time.

In 1856 Smetana accepted a post abroad. He took up an appointment as director of the Philharmonic Society of Gothenburg and spent a total of five years in Sweden where he conducted, played, and composed. Also during these years he visited his idol Liszt at Weimar.

By the early 1860s the political regime which followed the unsuccessful revolution of 1848 had become less strict. Smetana returned to Prague fired with a spirit of patriotism and was drawn towards opera.

In 1863 he completed his first—*The Brandenburgers in Bohemia*. The libretto (text) was written by the same author, the journalist Karel Sabina, who wrote that of *The Bartered Bride*.

Jealousies and accusations of 'Wagnerisms' in his music delayed his appointment as director of the Czech Provincial Theatre, later to become the National Theatre. He did, however, become conductor of one of the new choral societies and contributed a great deal to the organisation of Prague's musical life.

The National Theatre, Prague

Smetana entered *The Brandenburgers* for an opera competition. But various intrigues meant that the work itself was not staged until 1866—three years after its original date of completion. The work was highly successful. Smetana's supremacy on the Czech operatic scene was established when *The Bartered Bride* was given its first performance five months later. This double success silenced opposition, and in the autumn of 1866 Smetana was appointed Director of the National Opera in Prague.

Having composed some five operas Smetana's hearing began to deteriorate seriously. By the summer of 1872 he was almost completely deaf, with the consequence that he had to retire from the directorship of the National Opera. He had severe financial problems, but his generally optimistic spirit could not be easily dampened. For the next five years his activities revolved around composing six symphonic poems known as *Ma Vlast* (My Country). Smetana was generally recognized by the early 1880s as *the* great national composer. Celebrations were held to mark his half-century of music-making, and on 11 June 1881 another opera *Libuse* was performed on the opening night of the new National Theatre. It was again performed two years later when the theatre was re-opened after a disastrous fire which reduced the building to a heap of ashes only weeks after its original opening.

Smetana began work on one more opera—*Viola*—based on *Twelfth Night*, confirming a life-long love for the work of Shakespeare. A spell of mental depression turned to serious illness, and he died in a mental home on 12 May 1884.

The Bartered Bride became an important work for all those trying to establish a national Czech identity. Its village setting, with its chorus and dancers, were a constant source of inspiration. The story of the two young Czech people—the representatives of the new Czech spirit, cutting through the tangled web of debts, promises, and compromise with which their elders had shackled themselves—was highly appropriate. It symbolised the spirit of regeneration which was afoot in 1866. Jeník and Marenka, the lovers, demonstrate their independence by freeing themselves from past traditions and fight successfully for the right to decide their own future.

A view of Prague and the river Moldau in 1875

Kecal, the marriage broker (centre), with the lovers Marenka and Jeník, in a scene from the Sadler's Wells production of The Bartered Bride

GUIDE TO THE MUSIC

The story revolves around the rascally Kecal, a garrulous marriage-broker, who uses all his oily charm in the task of marrying Marenka to Vasek (the second son of a rich landowner, Tobias Micha). He does not know that Marenka is already in love with Jeník, a handsome stranger to the village.

Listen to: Overture

Its main theme is that used in the opera during the actual bartering.

ACT I

(*Scene: A square before an inn. Preparations have been made for a fair.*)

The annual church festival in a Czech village is in full swing, the villagers dancing and singing to celebrate the arrival of spring.

Listen to: (Chorus) 'See the buds burst on the bush'

Only Jeník, a poor young peasant, and Marenka, the daughter of rich farmer Krusina, are not happy. They are in love with each other. But Marenka has been ordered by her father to marry the stuttering Vasek, the son of the wealthy Micha. Marenka tells Jeník how much she loves him.

Listen to: Aria (Marenka) 'Gladly do I trust you'

Kecal, the sly marriage-broker, reminds Marenka's parents, Ludmilla and Krusina, that they have already legally contracted her to Tobias Micha's son, Vasek, whom he praises with cunning exaggeration in 'He's such a nice boy'.

Listen to: Trio (Ludmilla, Krusina, Kecal) 'As I said before old fellow'

The parents agree to sign the final deed; but Marenka protests passionately that she has a lover and, moreover, has 'never even seek Vasek'. Kecal's reaction to this bombshell is drowned in the exhilarating opening strains of the famous Polka which sweeps the act to a breathtaking, swirling finish.

Listen to: Polka

ACT II

(*Scene: Inside the inn.*)

The Furiant opens the second act, a drunken scene at the village inn.

Listen to: Furiant

Vasek sings, in a comic stutter, a song in which the music alternates between short and long notes, creating an irresistible effect.

Listen to: Aria (Vasek) 'Ma-Ma-Mamma so dear'

Marenka now enters the inn and craftily warns Vasek against the bride Kecal has picked out for him: she scares the timid Vasek off marrying 'that horrid girl Marenka', with tales of her flighty and spiteful character.

Listen to: Duet (Marenka, Vasek) 'Somewhere not so far away'

She then obtains from him a written promise that he will never marry that girl, and leaves. The inn empties except for Jeník and Kecal who now tries to bribe the young stranger to renounce Marenka for a rich widow—'She has a farm with sheep and meadows'.

Listen to: Duet (Kecal, Jeník) 'Just a moment if you please'

Jeník seems to be impressed by the promised dowry (of £4,000!), consents to renounce Marenka on the condition that *she marries only Micha's son*. Kecal takes this to mean Vasek, but Jeník is slyly referring to himself (for Jeník is Micha's son by his father's first marriage and has fled from home because of a wicked step-mother). As this arrangement fits Kecal's plans so exactly, he can hardly wait to summon the villagers to witness the deed.

ACT III

(*Scene: The square before the inn again.*)

A circus has come to the village and Vasek, especially, is overcome by the charms of Esmeralda, a tight-rope dancer. In a performance he plays the part of a bear, when his parents drag him away to his intended bride. By this time Marenka has learned that Jeník has given her up for £4,000, and she is naturally furious. She is told to 'think it over' by Kecal, her parents and prospective in-laws.

Listen to: Sextet (Ludmilla, Krusina, Hata, Micha, Marenka, Kecal)

In 'Our dream of love' she refuses to believe that Jeník could betray the love they share, for money.

Listen to: Recitative and Aria (Marenka) 'Our dream of love,

Jeník, finding her in tears cannot resist teasing her, and in her fury she vows to marry Vasek.

In the finale Kecal happily assembles the entire village to witness the success of his bridal arrangements, but Jeník appears and Tobias Micha recognises him as his long-lost son. Jeník now explains the trick he has played on Kecal: since Kecal's contract states that Marenka must marry the son of Micha, Jeník—the son of Micha—*can* be Marenka's husband. Marenka, reconciled, flings herself into the arms of Jeník, and Kecal leaves in angry humiliation as the villagers celebrate the new engagement.

Listen to: Finale (All) 'Well, well'

Nationalism in Czechoslovakia

A living language, spoken and written, results in a flourishing of literature and music, and the visual arts.

For over 200 years, since 1620, when it had lost its independence, the state of Czechoslovakia (then called Bohemia) had been a political and cultural desert. It had lost its national individuality.

The Czech language lived on only in villages, spoken by uneducated peasants who were looked down upon by the richer classes educated in German schools. But the descendants of these poor people dreamed of restoring the nation to its former glory.

At the beginning of the 19th century the government would not permit political organisations, and so national aspirations could only be encouraged through social gatherings where national songs and dances could be performed without interference from the government. Everyone sang the song 'Where is my homeland?' It symbolised the people's search for national identity, and later became Bohemia's National Anthem.

Despite the move towards reintroducing the Czech language German was the 'first language' for the first half of the last century. Smetana himself wrote his diaries in German, not Czech. These contain fascinating drawings and tell of his love and respect for village life and customs and of his love for dancing and dance tunes.

Smetana was particularly conscious of the lack of a distinctive, Czech music. He set out to fill the gap by composing operas, symphonies, chamber music, songs, piano pieces, and choral music.

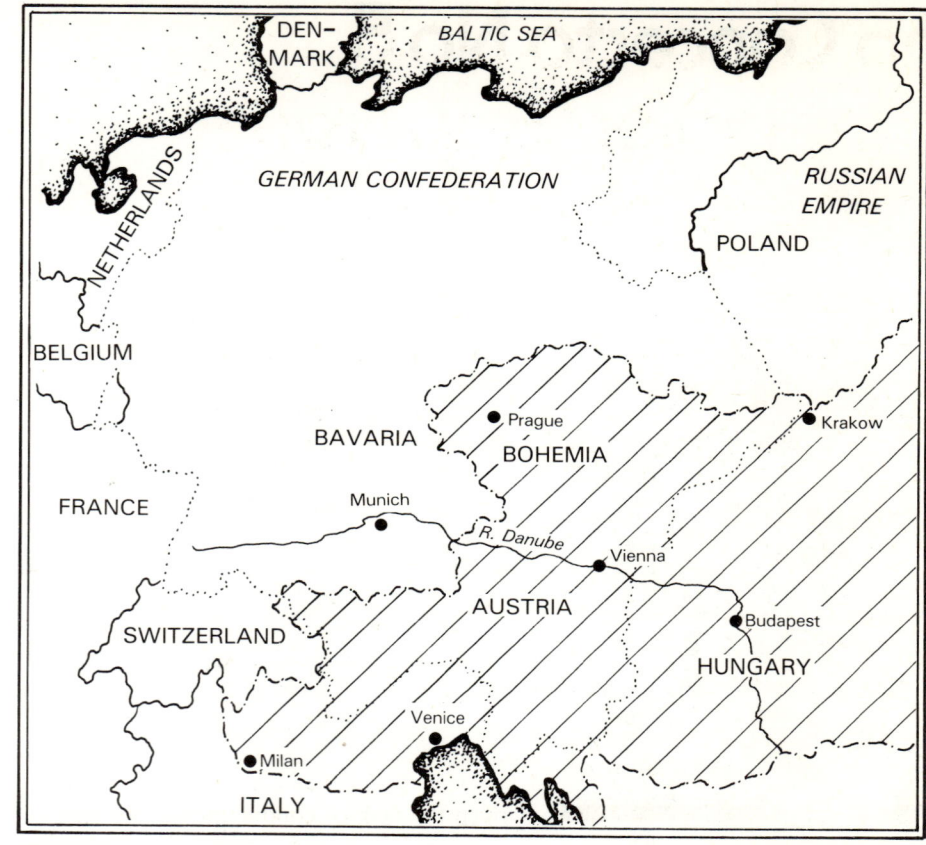

 Austrian Empire

Map showing Bohemia as part of the Austrian Empire in 1850

The circus manager from Act III of the opera

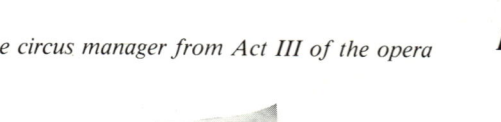 FOLLOW UP

1. Smetana was not the only composer to represent the nationalist movement in music. Which countries do you associate with these composers: Grieg; Sibelius; Dvořák; Mussorgsky? Find out the titles of some of the music they wrote and listen to it.
2. Listen to Smetana's symphonic poem *Vltava* and try to follow in musical terms the physical stages through which the great Bohemian river passes on its journey from source to sea. Can you spot any evidence of national musical characteristics in the piece?

Piano Concerto No 5 in E flat major (Emperor)

BY LUDWIG VAN BEETHOVEN (1770-1827)

Beethoven was born in Bonn, a city on the Rhine, which at that time was the seat of government of the Electorate of Cologne.

Beethoven's grandfather came to Bonn looking for a job as a musician and, being a man of some talent, he became director of music in the Elector's Chapel.

Beethoven's father was given an appointment as a tenor singer, but he turned out to be a drunkard and a bully. His wife was a quiet, affectionate woman, but without the strength to do much about the domestic problems caused by her husband. Seven children were born to the couple; Ludwig, the composer, was born in a room (now part of a Beethoven museum in Bonn) little larger than a garret.

Ludwig showed early signs of talent in music and his father set out to exploit this to make money. (Perhaps he was thinking of the young Mozart parading round Europe as a child prodigy.) Christian Neefe became Beethoven's teacher and guide and the 11-year-old Beethoven deputised for Neefe as court organist from time to time. In 1784 the Elector died and was succeeded by Maximilian Franz, an enlightened man who greatly liked music. In the same year Beethoven was appointed second court organist, and given the task of conducting at rehearsals.

In 1787 Beethoven went to Vienna to study. While he was there he had some lessons from Mozart. He soon returned to Bonn, however, to help out with domestic problems. At the same time he was becoming famous as a pianist and extemporiser. For four seasons he played viola in the Elector's theatre orchestra and in so doing learned a lot about all kinds of music, especially that of Mozart and Gluck.

Beethoven left Bonn in 1792 for a second time to go to Vienna and this time he stayed. He had composition lessons from Haydn, but these were not a great success.

Before Beethoven's time composers had been forced to rely on wealthy patrons to support them financially as they worked. Beethoven was the first composer to start composing and publishing music as a means of financial support. Patronage was a difficult idea for Beethoven to accept, and he certainly disliked the trappings of patronage—he didn't want to dress for dinner each day at 4.00 p.m.!

Musical composition came slowly for Beethoven. By the age of 30 only two or three of his major works had been composed. The laborious process by which his works developed is described in his sketch books. These provide a fascinating study of how the composer's mind actually worked through his ideas.

Signs of deafness first appeared in 1796, and by 1799 his hearing had deteriorated badly. In 1802 he took a holiday in Heiligenstadt to rest, and hopefully to recover. But by the autumn of that year he realised that deafness was about to overtake him. Incredibly, his spirit triumphed over this tragedy, and the majority of his works were composed after the onset of deafness.

Beethoven's music seemed revolutionary when compared with that of Mozart and Haydn which was being played throughout Europe around 1800. This is difficult for us to appreciate because we are in some ways 'conditioned' by the rich harmonies of Romantic music. The rhythmic irregularities of 20th-century music and the quest for new sounds in the 'pop' scene come between us and what it must have been like to hear Beethoven's music at first performance. People writing about his music then certainly commented on its forcefulness and disturbing qualities.

Beethoven's house in Bonn

GUIDE TO THE MUSIC

Beethoven wrote his fifth and last piano concerto in 1809-1810 and dedicated it to the Archduke Rudolph of Austria who was one of his pupils. The first performance took place in Leipzig on 28 November 1811.

FIRST MOVEMENT

Although by this time Beethoven was out of sympathy with Napoleon and the ideas he stood for, the title which has stuck with this concerto characterises the majestic opening of the first movement. In it the orchestra's boldly announced chords (E flat, A flat, B flat), interrupted by the piano's elaboration of them, outlines the key of E flat major like three massive columns supporting the whole movement.

The orchestral **exposition** lays out the themes from which the movement is constructed.

Theme A

The main theme from the group of **second subjects** is dramatically contrasting when first announced

Theme B

and takes on a smoother melodic shape as it is taken up by the horns.

Theme C

The closing section of the orchestral **exposition** is based on the triplet motif from Theme A and concludes with:

The piano introduces the second **exposition** material with an upward rising chromatic scale ending in a trill. The piano's exposition of Theme A is dignified, quiet and restrained before it plunges into passage work. After the reappearance of the second subject the closing section offers another opportunity for the display of virtuosity.

The **development** is based mainly on the triplet motif from Theme A. It reaches a climax in the passage between orchestra and piano played *ff*. The triplet figure in the lower strings together with music of Theme C begins quietly, and, as the volume and emotional intensity increase, they herald the beginning of the **recapitulation**.

The **recapitulation** restates first and second subjects. At the point where it would be normal for the soloist to perform a **cadenza** (either of his own composition, or by the composer of the piece), there is a pause over the orchestral chord and Beethoven has written an instruction to the soloist to proceed directly to the Coda.

A brief bridge passage on the piano leads to the Coda or tail piece of the movement which begins quietly with a reference to the second subject before a downward chromatic scale leads to some forceful music based on Theme A.

SECOND MOVEMENT

Muted strings give out the following theme:

Beethoven sketched the theme in many forms before he reached what he considered to be entirely appropriate. Compare the final version with these 'trials'.

The middle section consists of a series of slowly descending curves for the solo piano.

The music repeats the first section of the movement and continues its flow of delicate and beautiful inspiration until it finally ends in B major. Bassoons sustain the note B. They sink a semitone to B flat. This note is now sustained by the horns and over this the piano wafts a magical phrase. After a brief pause we are plunged into—

THIRD MOVEMENT

The music at the end of the slow movement turns out to be the basis of the **rondo** theme which recurs throughout the movement.

The first episode introduces two new thematic ideas.

Shortly the rondo theme occurs again.

The second episode takes the form of a development section where elements of the rondo theme and its closing phrases are worked on.

The rondo theme occurs for the third time at the beginning of a repetition of all the earlier material used in the movement. To the accompaniment of the rhythm repeated over and over in the timpani the piano solo gradually dies away. It disappears almost to nothing before, as if rising from the ashes, vigorous scales from the soloist bring the movement to a climax with a final repetition of the original rondo theme.

Beethoven playing to his friends

The concerto

There are three movements in a concerto:
1. A fast movement—often marked *allegro*.
2. A slow, song-like movement—perhaps marked *andante* or *adagio*.
3. A fast movement (finale)—often marked *allegro*.

The first movement of a concerto is generally in Sonata Form (see *Portraits in Music 1*, page 20). But in the concertos of the Mozart-Beethoven period there is sometimes what is called a **double exposition**. As the name implies, the themes of the exposition are heard twice, first played by the orchestra and second played by the orchestra and soloist. The repetition is of course not exact, partly because the purpose of the two sections is different. The aim of the first exposition is to set out the basic themes of the movement and to establish firmly its sense of key. The second exposition is always in the same key as the first, i.e. the home key.

Cadenza

To a certain extent 'The Emperor' is not typical of its period in that it lacks a **cadenza** at the traditional places in the concerto—towards the close of the first and final movements. After a sustained orchestral build-up leading to a pause there was an opportunity for the soloist to show off his technical ability on his instrument and his powers of improvisation. This is called a **cadenza**. Later 19th-century composers wrote out their cadenzas in full because they were afraid of soloists spoiling the effect of the music by inventing unsuitable cadenzas.

FOLLOW UP

| MOZART | SCHUMANN | LISZT | RACHMANINOV |
| 1756-91 | 1810-56 | 1811-86 | 1873-1943 |

The above composers all composed popular piano concertos. Choose a concerto (or part of one) by one of these composers, listen to it and compare it with *The Emperor*. Which do you like best?

Beethoven at work in his study

PETRUSHKA

BALLET

BY IGOR STRAVINSKY (1882-1971)

Stravinsky is one of the most important composers of the 20th century. His life was spent moving westwards in an attempt to find a tranquil setting in which to make music. Exiled from Russia in 1917 by the October Revolution, he first went to Switzerland, and then France, before moving on to America at the outbreak of World War II. Having become a French citizen in 1934 he then became a naturalised American and lived in Hollywood, a far cry from his native Russia.

Igor Stravinsky was born in 1882 at Oranienbaum, near St. Petersburg (now Leningrad). His father was a bass singer at the Imperial Opera House. In his conversations with the American musician and writer Robert Craft, the physical and emotional details of Stravinsky's childhood are recorded with great clarity; his father was impatient, authoritarian, and punished his four sons to the point of cruelty. Stravinsky felt lonely and unloved by his parents as a child, and the cell of Petrushka, the puppet character of Stravinsky's ballet, was based on the composer's memory of his own bedroom in his parent's home.

He was 'encouraged' by his parents to study law, but in 1902 he showed some of his compositions to Rimsky-Korsakov at the University. The composer agreed to accept him as a private pupil—on condition he undertook remedial work in harmony and counterpoint!

In his teacher's home he met many influential people of St. Petersburg, among them Diaghilev, the director of the Ballet Russe. The latter asked the young composer to orchestrate two pieces by Chopin for the Ballet Russe. The resulting ballets were then performed in Paris in 1909. Diaghilev, three artistic advisers, and Stravinsky were soon at work on projects for the 1910 season. For this Stravinsky wrote the music of *The Firebird; Petrushka* followed in 1911, and with Nijinsky and Karsavina as the leading dancers, Stravinsky's fame soon spread widely.

In his music, as in life, Stravinsky was quick to respond to changes, and new developments were assimilated into his music freely. Stravinsky's later music was very varied (one piano concerto, one piano sonata, one violin concerto, one mass, and so on). However, in his youth he concentrated largely on ballet. The three Russian ballets commissioned by Diaghilev were: *The Firebird* (1909), *Petrushka* (1910-11), and *The Rite of Spring* (1911-13).

Stravinsky with the dancer Nijinsky as Petrushka

GUIDE TO THE MUSIC

Petrushka, according to Stravinsky, was originally inspired by a vision he had while working on a piece for piano solo and orchestra. In the composer's own words:

> *I had in my mind a distinct picture of a puppet, suddenly endowed with life, exasperating the patience of the orchestra with diabolic cascades of arpeggios. The orchestra retaliates . . . The outcome is a terrific noise . . . and ends in the sorrowful collapse of the poor puppet.*

Diaghilev persuaded Stravinsky to change his plans and turn the orchestral piece into a ballet, dramatising the idea of a puppet's suffering.

The action takes place on the Admiralty Square, St. Petersburg, in the 1830s. Besides the normal theatre curtain there is a special curtain for the Burlesque (parody). This curtain pictures a Charlatan of magnificent appearance enthroned on the clouds. (A Charlatan is a character who is an impostor, pretending to have great knowledge or skill.) The ordinary curtain goes up immediately the music has begun and falls at the end of the ballet. The special curtain goes up a little later and falls between the scenes.

FIRST SCENE *The Shrovetide Fair*

A sunny winter's day. On the left a large booth with a balcony for the 'Diède' (compère of the fair). Underneath it is a table with an enormous samovar. In the middle of the scene is the little theatre of the Charlatan, on the right there are sweetmeat stalls and a showman of optical illusions. At the back one sees a roundabout with wooden horses, big swings and slides. There is a crowd of people moving about on the scene, common people, gentlefolk, troupes of drunkards with their arms round one another; the stall of the optical illusionist is surrounded by children; women are clustered round the other booths.

The opening bars of music suggest the colourful crowd bustling about excitedly.

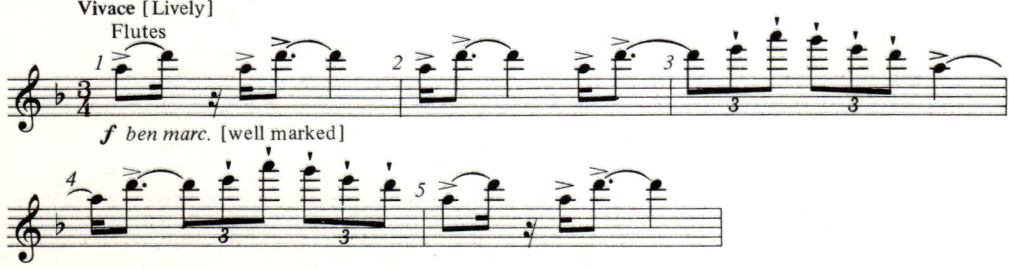

This flute melody is accompanied by two horns and two clarinets. Interest transfers to the accompanying figure, and soon a brief motif (theme) appears in the bass instruments.

This is taken over by the whole orchestra and provides the accompaniment for the passing-by of a group of drunken men.

The noise of the fair goes on while the crowd gathers on stage to music ending in:

An organ-grinder joins the gathering accompanied by his lady dancer who pirouettes to the strains of a merry tune played on the barrel-organ. (While he was working on the score of *Petrushka* Stravinsky had actually heard this tune played on a barrel-organ.)

In his ingenious orchestration Stravinsky suggests the creaking of the barrel-organ mechanism through his writing for piccolo and flute.

Another street musician arrives, also with a dancer, and on his musical box he plays a French dance tune.

As the dancers perform in competition with one another their respective tunes are heard in combination. When the crowd begins to move off again the opening theme is heard once more.

After a climax is reached a loud drum roll draws attention to the fact that the Showman has appeared outside his booth and that the curtain of the puppet theatre is about to rise. The Showman produces a flute and begins to play a cadenza (solo passage) finishing with three fragments:

The people gathering to watch the puppet theatre with the Moor, the Ballerina and Petrushka

This tells the crowd that the instrument is a magic flute. As the curtain rises his three puppets appear: **Petrushka**, the **Ballerina** and the **Moor**. He touches each in turn with his flute, the puppets come to life and join in a vigorous Russian dance, all this to the joy and amazement of the crowd.

This brings the opening scene to an end.

SECOND SCENE *In Petrushka's Room*

Percussions roll. Its cardboard walls are painted black with stars and a half moon. Drawings of devils on a golden background decorate the panels of the door which leads into the Ballerina's room. On one of the walls of the cell is a frowning portrait of the Charlatan, below it and a little to one side Petrushka, in a paroxysm of despair, is digging a hole.

The door opens and the Showman kicks Petrushka into a corner of the room where he lies cursing with rage. Petrushka is a tragic figure. Despite the fact that he is made with sawdust he is the most human of the three puppets because he knows the pain of suffering and rejection. He loves the Ballerina but she doesn't respond because she finds him too ugly. He picks himself up and begins to dance:

Clarinet I part can be played on the 'white' keys only of the piano while clarinet II part uses only 'black' keys—R.H. underneath and L.H. on top. Petrushka's theme played in this way suggests the puppet's clashing feelings of love and rejection.

All of a sudden the Ballerina appears. Attracted to the Moor, she passes Petrushka's cell and for a moment his spirits are raised. When he realises she is indifferent to him he bursts out in anger, portrayed in the orchestra by dissonant brass sounds.

THIRD SCENE *The Moor's Room*

The wall is papered with a pattern of green palms and fantastic fruits on a red background. The Moor, dressed in a costume of the greatest splendour, is lying on a low sofa playing with a coconut. On the right is a door which leads into the Ballerina's cell.

The Moor at first dances rather clumsily and then more vigorously, trying unsuccessfully to split the coconut with his sword. The Moor's dance tune is exotic and its subtle rhythms are brought out by the accompaniment of soft percussion instruments.

The Moor's dance is interrupted by the arrival of the Ballerina who dances to a light, swiftly moving tune played by solo trumpet with snare drum accompaniment. The music suddenly changes to a waltz, slow at first, then gradually speeding up. The Moor is enchanted with her appearance and tries to join in but finds that the steps of his previous dance will not fit!

Petrushka's motif, heard on the trumpet, heralds his appearance. Dissonant harmonies portray his anger and jealousy on finding the Ballerina with the Moor. The latter fights Petrushka off with his sword and eventually throws him out of the room.

FOURTH SCENE *The Shrovetide Fair* (Evening)

> The same scenery as in the first scene. Towards the end an effect of late evening. On the appearance of the mummers, Bengal lights are lit in the wings. At the moment of Petrushka's death it begins to snow and the darkness becomes deeper.

Back in the colour and bustle of the square of St. Petersburg a group of nursemaids perform a dance.

The pace of the merrymaking builds up: a peasant with a performing bear begins to dance and tries to imitate him; a wealthy merchant with more money than sense throws banknotes to the crowd; the coachmen, also popular figures in Russian carnivals, join in the dancing and are followed by a group of masqueraders, one disguised as the devil, one as a goat, and another as a pig.

There are sounds of disturbance from the Showman's booth. Everyone's attention is turned to the puppet theatre. Petrushka dashes out, closely pursued by the Moor with sword in hand. Petrushka's motif is heard one last last time before the Moor catches up with him and cuts him down with his sword. The Showman carries off his dead body towards the theatre with the assurance to the crowd that his characters are no more than puppets.

The crowd disperses. The Showman is left alone in the gathering darkness. Suddenly, the ghost of Petrushka appears eerily above the puppet theatre and the terrified Showman drops Petrushka, the puppet dummy, and dashes in fear from the square.

FOLLOW UP

Using instruments available in the classroom try to make up a piece of Fairground Music. Ideas for musical illustration—either singly or in combination—might include:

- Roundabout
- Shooting stall
- Swings
- Cries of showmen
- Fairground in the evening—bright lights

Through Adam's Fall

CHORALE PRELUDE
BY J. S. BACH (1685-1750)

Johann Sebastian Bach was born in 1685 in Eisenach, in East Germany. Bach's father was a town musician of Eisenach and died when Bach was only ten. The young boy was taken into the household of his elder brother from whom he received keyboard instruction, and also began his lifelong habit of copying out and studying other composers' music.

The young Bach did well at school and sang in both school and church choirs. Aged 15 he travelled north to Lüneburg and joined the choir of St. Michael's Church. While there, Bach walked the 30 miles to Hamburg to hear the celebrated organist Reinken play. In 1702 Bach took up a post as violinist in the court of Weimar and in the following year became organist at Arnstadt. In 1705 he travelled north again, this time to study with the composer Buxtehude and enjoyed playing on the magnificent organ made by Schnitger in Buxtehude's church.

He was reprimanded for staying away from Arnstadt for too long and, unhappy with the prospects in his present post, took up an appointment as organist at Mülhausen in 1707. He didn't stay there long, however, moving within a year to become chamber musician and court organist at Weimar where his duties were divided between the court orchestra and those of organist of the Castle Church.

Bach had already written music for the organ at Arnstadt and Mülhausen. At Weimar, where the organ was larger, his music for the instrument took on a grander style, and he began to compose preludes, fugues and other pieces.

In 1717 Bach became Kapellmeister (chief musician) to the court at Cöthen and there composed the majority of his chamber music: *Brandenburg Concertos*, orchestral suites, concertos, and sonatas.

The tragic death of his first wife, coupled with an increasing disinterest in music on the part of his patron, encouraged Bach to look around for a new post. This time he was appointed Cantor to St. Thomas's Church, Leipzig in 1723. His time there was not happy and there were continuing problems between himself and the officials of the church, town, and university. Nevertheless he spent 25 years in this post. At Leipzig he wrote some of his greatest works: the *Magnificat*, the *St. Matthew Passion*, the *Mass in B Minor*, *Goldberg Variations*, *The Musical Offering* and *The Art of Fugue*.

Bach went blind in 1749. His death followed shortly after an unsuccessful eye operation in 1750.

FAMOUS ORGAN BUILDERS

The North German organs, in particular those of **Schnitger** in Hamburg and Lübeck, made a lasting impression on J. S. Bach. As instruments they had great potential for the virtuoso organist and certainly influenced the scope and nature of Bach's organ music. One of the features of Bach's life you will have noticed is that he moved to different posts quite frequently during his lifetime. His organ music reflects these changes in its variety of style and technical demands. In his years at Leipzig he was equally influenced by what might be called the Southern School of organ builders, chief among whom were Andreas and Gottfried **Silbermann**. They combined in their instruments the best features of French, Italian, and German organ building traditions.

Map showing the places where Bach lived

GUIDE TO THE MUSIC

For use during church services Bach wrote two types of music for organ based on chorale (hymn) tunes: variations on a chorale melody, played between the verses of the hymn sung by the congregation or else settings of the chorale tune during which it is heard only once. This latter type, known as **chorale preludes**, feature in an important collection dating from Bach's Weimar and Cöthen periods known as the *Little Organ Book*.

'Through Adam's fall mankind fell too' is taken from this collection and the music is based on a chorale tune which appeared in a mid-16th-century religious song book.

The words of the hymn are by Spengler (1479-1534) and have been translated from the German as follows. (The translation's end-of-line rhymes are slightly distracting, but at least the message is clear!)

> *When Adam fell, the frame entire*
>   *Of nature was infected;*
> *The source whence came the poison dire*
>   *Was not to be corrected;*
> *The lust accursed, indulged at first,*
>   *Brought death as its production;*
> *But God's free grace hath saved our race*
>   *From misery and destruction.*

As you might expect, the mood of Bach's setting is sombre—to reflect the gloom and doom of the poem. Despite the look of the music—it has almost continuous semiquavers—the speed of the music is slow. Both the **manual** parts (top two staves—upper for right hand and lower for left hand) and the **pedal** part contain a considerable number of sharps and flats. This **chromaticism** together with the 'falling' motif (theme) in the pedals contributes to the mood.

Notice how the chorale tune remains undecorated in the highest part. In the accompanying parts notes are frequently sharpened or flattened, then the flat or sharp is cancelled. Look at the opening five notes of the piece.

These 'contradictions' are combined with falling intervals in the pedal part in a way which increases the emotional content of the music. Some people have said that the 'falling seventh' motif is symbolic of Adam's and mankind's fall. But this is perhaps reading too much into the music.

Bach's setting is a fine example of **counterpoint** (the combining of two or more melodic lines). Each part has a melodic life of its own. To become thoroughly familiar with this music listen to it several times and each time try to follow a different individual part.

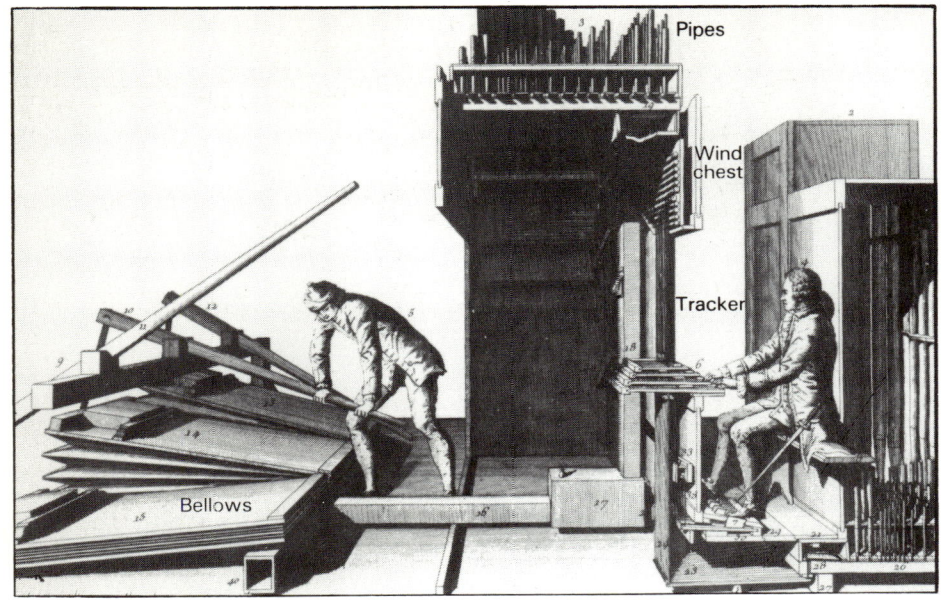

Diagram showing tracker action

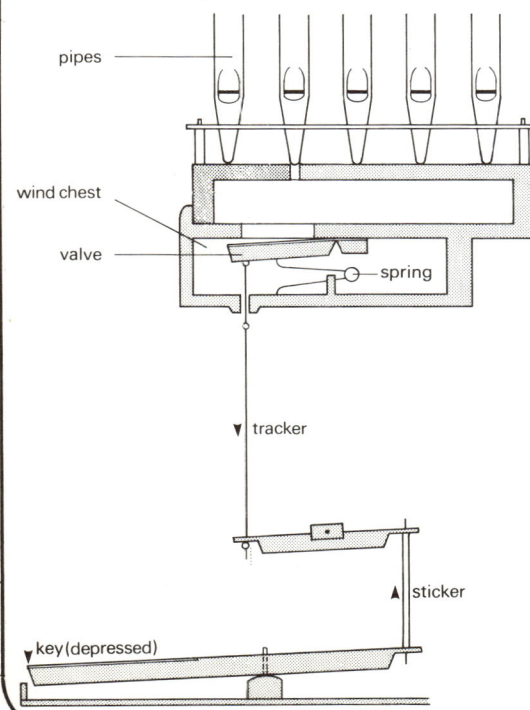

The organ

The organ is an immensely complicated instrument. In simple terms the manuals, played by the hands, and the pedal board, played by the feet, control the flow of air into the pipes placed in rows on top of a large wind chest within the organ case. In early instruments the various sections of the organ were separated in the pipe case according to their function (e.g. pedal pipes all grouped together). The player used a system of levers called **trackers** and **stickers** to make direct contact with the pipes. This kind of action was known as **tracker action.** Bach composed for organs of this type. There are two basic kinds of pipe in an organ (a) **flue pipes** (the air passes over a lip as in the recorder) and (b) **reed pipes** (in which the air is forced through a reed as on the clarinet).

St. Thomas's Church, Leipzig and (inset) a portrait of the composer

1. Try to arrange a visit to a local church which has a pipe organ and either with your teacher or the organist see a demonstration of the instrument. Then ask for an explanation of the following: manuals, pedal board, stops, swell-box, flues, reeds, mixture, coupling, registration, tremulant.

2. Listen to other examples of J. S. Bach's chorale preludes. Besides the example we have studied there are two other main varieties. The first, sometimes called a *canto fermo* chorale, has the tune played in long notes on the pedal; the second has the tune elaborately ornamented and decorated in the top part with more simple accompanying parts. See if you can spot examples of all three types in the music you listen to.

SYMPHONY NO. 2 (The Four Temperaments)

BY CARL NIELSEN (1865-1931)

Carl Nielsen was born in Copenhagen in 1865. He was the son of a poor house-painter who played the violin at local village dances to earn some extra money. When Carl was six he caught measles and was confined to the house; to entertain him his mother sang folk songs and the young boy tried to copy these on the violin. His musical talent was soon obvious and his parents sent him to violin lessons. But Carl was more interested in learning to play the trumpet and when about fifteen he joined a military band.

His musical ability gained him a place at the Copenhagen Conservatory where his teacher, Niels Gade, described his early compositions as 'a muddle—but a talented muddle.'

To earn a living he became a second violinist with the Royal Theatre and in the meantime carried on his studies. He sometimes felt bitter about having to eke out a living in the orchestral pit at times when he was desperate to compose. His circumstances contrasted sharply with those of another great Scandinavian musician, Sibelius, who was composing with the aid of grants from the Finnish government. Nielsen's days as a second violinist ended in 1908 when he was appointed conductor of the very orchestra in which he had been playing. In 1915 he became Director of the Conservatory in Copenhagen and until his death in 1931 he wrote music and taught students with great enthusiasm. Nielsen is chiefly known for his six symphonies, the *Helios* Overture, a Flute Concerto and a Violin Concerto. Contrary to many of the trends in 20th-century music Nielsen's work is straight-forward, sometimes grand and stirring, sometimes eloquent and moving. The general mood of most of Nielsen's works is optimistic. He made no secret of the fact that he despised many of the modern trends in music; he hated Schoenberg's experiments with atonality and was unimpressed by Stravinsky's later works.

Carl Nielsen's study

GUIDE TO THE MUSIC

Eight years after the composition of his first symphony Nielsen himself conducted the first performance of Symphony No. 2 (The Four Temperaments) in 1902. The idea for the symphony came to him in a village pub in Zealand. In the saloon where he was drinking beer with his wife and some friends, there hung a comical picture. It was in four sections and showed the temperaments with the titles: The Choleric, The Phlegmatic, The Melancholic and The Sanguine. The choleric man was on horseback: he had a long sword in his hand with which he slashed widely at the empty air, his eyes were nearly rolling out of his head and his hair flew madly round his face. The other three pictures were in the same style and their exaggerated expressions and comical gravity greatly amused Nielsen.

The images stayed in his memory and he later decided to depict the various moods in musical terms.

FIRST MOVEMENT

(Allegro collerico)

This movement begins with an impetuous theme:

A contrasting lively phrase on the clarinet soon emerges.

In the composer's own words the music proceeds 'now wildly and impetuously, like one who nearly forgets himself, now in softer mood, like one who regrets his bad temper'.

SECOND MOVEMENT

(*Allegro comodo and flemmattico*)

This movement takes the shape of a leisurely waltz.

When he was writing this music Nielsen was thinking of a young lad, loved by everyone. In school he was popular with everyone, but the teachers were at the same time in despair for he was always behind with his school work. He simply wanted to spend all his time lying on the pier at the harbour, with his legs dangling over the edge. Only once is the mood disturbed. Did a barrel fall into the harbour from a ship, disturbing the boy lying on the pier dreaming? Maybe. So what? In a moment everything is quiet again. The lad falls asleep, the world dozes, and the water is again smooth as a mirror.

Nielsen with his family

THIRD MOVEMENT

(*Allegro malinconico*)

This movement, says Nielsen, tries to express the basic character of a heavy melancholy man.

However, there is pain here in addition to suffering and sadness and this is expressed in a haunting oboe melody.

After a massive climax the music sinks to rest.

FOURTH MOVEMENT

(*Allegro sanguineo*)

The sanguine man does not give a care for the world; he sees no difficulties because he has never had any in his life. His rough strength is coupled with hearty laughter.

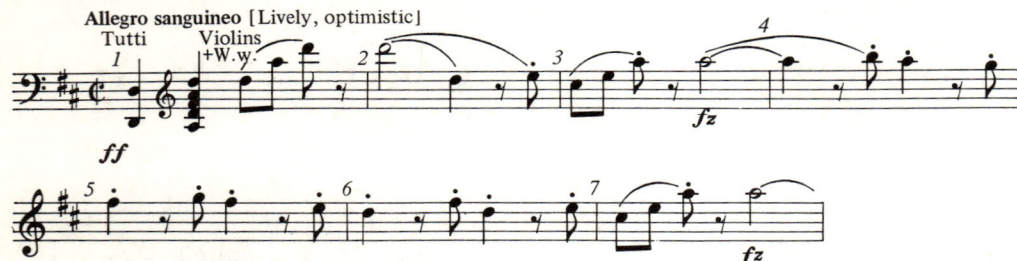

This is music of a man who believes the world belongs to him, and in Nielsen's words 'that fried pigeons will fly into his mouth without work or bother.'

Something scares him, however, but not for long. The superficial mood of brash cheeriness returns. The march which rounds off the movement, though lively, is more dignified and perhaps his fright—whatever it was—has made the man more thoughtful.

The Four Temperaments

In psychology, temperament is a term used in describing the prevailing mood of a person. A Greek physician who lived in the 2nd century A.D. developed the idea of temperament from an earlier theory based on the assumption that there were four basic body fluids (humours): blood, phlegm, black bile and yellow bile. These fluids, depending on their relative strengths in the individual, were believed to produce respectively **temperaments** labelled **sanguine** (warm, pleasant), **phlegmatic** (sluggish, apathetic), **melancholic** (depressed, sad), and **choleric** (quick to react, hot-tempered). This theory was the first of many efforts to group human beings into types. Even today, scientists believe that the chemicals produced by certain glands have an influence on emotional reactions.

FOLLOW UP

1. Find out what you can about Schoenberg's methods of composition which so antagonised Nielsen. To start you off on your hunt look up a music dictionary for an explanation of **atonality** and **serialism.**

2. Grieg and Sibelius were two Scandinavian composers who also portrayed people, places and events in their music. Find out something about Grieg and Sibelius and listen to music from Grieg's *Peer Gynt* Suite and Sibelius's tone poem *Finlandia*.

Nielsen (far left) playing first violin (the leader) in a string quartet

Grieg (1843-1907). Norwegian composer

Sibelius (1865-1957). Finnish composer